Whatever Comes
EAT IT

Living and working as an expat in **Russia**, **Bangladesh**, **Thailand**, **UAE** and **South Korea**

by **Kathy Binns**

 FriesenPress

One Printers Way
Altona, MB R0G 0B0
Canada

www.friesenpress.com

ISBN
978-1-03-915840-5 (Hardcover)
978-1-03-915839-9 (Paperback)
978-1-03-915841-2 (eBook)

1. BIOGRAPHY & AUTOBIOGRAPHY, PERSONAL MEMOIRS

Distributed to the trade by The Ingram Book Company

*I dedicate this book to my father, Bernard,
husband, Michael and daughter, Elizabeth*

Table of Contents

Preface

"It's Tuesday, it must be Belgium"

I worked overseas as an expatriate, or foreign national, for seventeen years from 2004-2021. During this time, I taught at international schools in Moscow, Bangladesh, Thailand, the UAE, and South Korea. Living and working overseas was a unique lifestyle. Well-established, English speaking expat bubbles existed in all the places I worked. These expat bubbles enabled teachers, business people, and other workers to get by with minimal knowledge of the local language. Specific grocery stores, bars, and restaurants supported our daily needs. Staff spoke English and products were imported from around the world.

Outside the expat bubble life was very different. My ability to be flexible and see humour in situations helped me navigate through many tense moments. Miming and translation books and apps were essential. My stories of buying food and ordering at restaurants will resonate with anyone who has traveled to foreign countries.

For teachers working, or considering work overseas, this book is full of survival tips, good advice about the selection process, and what to look for when being interviewed. I describe the housing arrangements I experienced as well as the process of getting work visas and travel documents. As a teacher of biology and as the head of the science department I witnessed first-hand how educational philosophies influenced teaching and learning inside and outside of the classroom. Acquisition of supplies was an issue in all the schools I worked at. A wide spectrum of attitudes towards health and safety made life challenging at times.

I describe my experiences with dental services as well as hospitalizations in Moscow, Bangladesh and South Korea. Negotiating the private medical insurance systems provided by the schools was enlightening as Canada has a universal, government supported system.

My family, expatriate teaching colleagues, and nursing friends encouraged me to write this book. Various real individuals appear within the text. I have either changed their names, or omitted surnames to safeguard their privacy. I could not include all my experiences, so I focus on the more memorable and unique. Living inside and outside the expat bubble was never boring.

Opportunity

In 2004 I had no complaints. My twenty-two-year-old daughter was living independently, and I had a successful career as an acute care registered nurse and clinical nursing instructor. Michael, my second husband, and I were using sabbaticals to complete our Master of Education at the University of Victoria in British Columbia, Canada. Michael was a middle school band teacher, and we had met playing badminton at a community club in the town of Courtenay, British Columbia.

While in Victoria our mutual desire to live and work in different countries led us to investigate short term overseas jobs. England, Australia, and New Zealand were the obvious choices as our credentials were recognized and the spoken language was English. An international nursing shortage meant that short-term nursing positions in the US, UK and Australia were posted in newspapers and jobs for me were plentiful and well-paying. Finding a suitable teaching job for Michael was not as simple. The British recruiters we spoke to were looking for teachers willing to work in inner cities for low wages. The conditions were attractive to new graduates on supply lists, but not to well-paid permanent teachers.

When the opportunity to teach at an international school in Moscow came available, we took it. Michael would teach music, but I had to change careers from recovery room nurse and clinical instructor to teaching middle school science. The switch was not difficult as I held bachelor degrees in education and nursing as well as my new master's in education. In addition, I had taught medical office assistants as well as clinical skills to nursing students.

Working as teachers overseas was rewarding and our teaching schedules provided holidays in the fall, winter and spring. During holidays we traveled and explored a number of European and Asian countries as well as Australia and New Zealand. In the summers Michael and I returned to Canada and talked to our friends about what it was like to live overseas—about the differences in culture and politics and how these affected the basic infrastructure of a society. Public systems of health care, electricity and water were not universal, and we gained a better appreciation of the social benefits of Canada's democratic government and the underlying collectiveness of our society.

The expatriate life satisfied our desire to see the world, and we learned not to judge behaviours that were unfamiliar. Over the years it became apparent that there was no "right way" to do things. Living in English speaking bubbles created by international schools and the services that supported them were very different from living as citizens. Michael and I were functionally illiterate foreign nationals in all the countries in which we lived. Often daily living was challenging, but always memorable.

Chapter 1:
The Beginning: Russia
2004-2009

"A truly happy person is one who can enjoy the scenery on a detour."

-Gregory Benford-

One evening in February 2004, Michael was checking his emails when he found one from his former spouse. After no contact for years she had felt the need to tell him that she was leaving the country to teach music in China. Her email intrigued Michael. She mentioned that she had declined a job offer from a school in Moscow to accept the China job.

Michael emailed back asking if she would share the Moscow contact, and she replied within minutes. Unbeknownst to me, Michael immediately phoned the Anglo-American school of Moscow to express his interest in the position. He discovered that the recruiter was staying at a hotel in Vancouver. Michael called the hotel and reached the principal in his room. He was happy to talk to Michael about the music position, as it was still available.

At the time I assumed Michael was talking to a recruiting agent from the United Kingdom we had been corresponding with. At one point in the conversation, Michael said, "I don't know, why don't you ask her yourself," and he handed me the phone.

The man on the line asked if I could teach science to middle school students. I said "Yes." The topic of cold and dark winters came up. I told him I had grown up in Winnipeg, at which point he told me that his wife was from Kenora. I knew people from Kenora, and we discovered that we had a mutual acquaintance. A friend of mine was his wife's mother's best friend. Six degrees of separation had socially connected us within the first few minutes of our conversation.

I liked the principal immediately. Even though I did not know which school he worked for we arranged to meet in Richmond, B.C., for a face-to-face interview the coming weekend. Once I hung up, Michael told me that the music teacher's job was at the Anglo-American school in Moscow, Russia.

Our recruitment process was a bit unorthodox as it was late in the hiring season for international schools. We had not used a recruiting agency, but had become aware of the vacancy by word of mouth. The interview itself was on the weekend at a public school in Richmond where a friend of the principal worked. At the interview the principal, who had a great sense of humor, asked why we wanted to leave the beauty of British Columbia. The sun was shining, and the snow-capped mountains could be seen in the distance. We laughed and told him it was the first time we had seen sun and blue sky in months.

A week after our interview we were offered two-year teaching contracts. The decision to move overseas was easy; it was what we wanted in the short term. After accepting the positions all the pieces fell into place quickly. Our decision to pack up everything and leave Canada felt like it was "meant to be." We rented our house in Comox within a week. My parents were happy to let us store our possessions in their basement. We were both granted leaves from our Canadian jobs, and I arranged for the final exam for my University of Victoria Masters of Education degree to be written in Moscow in September.

On a whim Michael and I borrowed a video from the public library about life in Russia. The video dated from the late 1990s and showed people lining up with small bags trying to purchase eggs and bread. The food was obviously being rationed, and the people looked stressed. Luckily, the video was not even close to the reality of living in Russia in the early 2000s.

Michael and I knew that living and working in Moscow was going to be interesting from many perspectives. In addition, the location would give us easy access to Europe for holidays. What we had not planned on was staying overseas for seventeen years.

******

Arriving in Moscow

When the principal asked us not to judge Moscow by the airport we thought it was a strange thing to say until we walked through it. Even though Sheremetyevo was one of the busiest airports in Europe, in 2004 its internal and external decorations dated from the 1960's. The whole building retained the feel of the Soviet era. In particular, the ceilings were dark brown with strange circle installations, similar to upside-down coffee cans. The dark color of the ceiling made the rooms oppressive and not very inviting, a stark contrast to the brightly lit Vancouver airport with its totem poles and waterfalls.

In addition to strange decoration choices, passport control had not been designed or renovated to cope with increasing numbers of travelers. When we arrived at Sheremetyevo we stood in individual lines in front of each booth. It was "luck of the draw" as to which line was going to be the quickest. We immediately appreciated the long single line system, which allowed the first in line the next available customs agent.

Going through Russian customs was a bit stressful as we only knew a few words of Russian and the customs agents usually did not know English. The school provided a cheat sheet to help us fill out the landing papers required to enter the country. These documents helped us get through passport control on the way in.

In Russia the examination of passports was the same when entering and leaving the country. The requirements for Russians to leave were much higher than those we needed to leave Canada. Michael and I saw many travelers being taken to back rooms if their paperwork was deemed out of order. Teacher friends had experienced this firsthand when one of their passports had water damage from being dropped in the snow. They were not allowed to leave the country until their embassy confirmed that their passport and Russian work visa were indeed valid. We learned to plan for difficulties with passport control, and always arrived at the airport earlier than required.

When returning from trips Michael and I looked for lines that were free of foreign travelers as they always seemed to have something wrong with their paperwork. In addition to foreign passport paperwork delays, women with young children walked directly to the front of the lines to jump the queue. The behavior was accepted by everyone, and it seemed to be the decent thing to do as the children were usually crying. No one wanted to listen to crying children while waiting in line.

******

When Michael and I first arrived in Moscow we nervously followed the crowd. Once through customs were met at the baggage carousels by the schools welcoming team. While we waited for other teachers to make their way through customs, we were given an envelope with a substantial number of rubles. The money was to be used to buy groceries and other necessities before our first month's pay was deposited into the American bank account we had set up before we left Canada.

We were told that it was impossible to exchange Canadian dollars, and that there was only one automatic bank machine that was trustworthy in the city. The machine, guarded by a security man, was located downtown close to the Kutz building complex where many teachers and embassy staff were housed. Any other international bank machines in the city were likely connected to fraud schemes, and it was strongly suggested that we did not use them. Michael and I found it inconvenient to drive down to this bank machine. We were grateful that within a few months of our arrival the school installed automatic bank machines inside the school. Michael and I withdrew enough cash to buy food and gas biweekly. We got accustomed to carrying large amounts of cash.

******

The airport waiting area was busy and chaotic. A group of unofficial taxi drivers continually called out to travelers coming from the baggage area. Our greeters told us that these drivers were known to charge too much money and took foreigners on joy rides to increase the fares. While we worked there the Anglo-American School provided vans and drivers for us to get to and from the airports because of the lack of trustworthy public transport. By the late 2000s metro lines had reached the major airports and teachers used this means of transport when convenient.

Once the remaining teachers in our group arrived, we walked outside to find the school van parked on the sidewalk just outside the entrance. Although illegal in Canada, we were to find that parking on sidewalks was common practice in Moscow as well as other countries.

Sheremetyevo airport was located twenty-eight kilometers north of the center of Moscow. After leaving the airport, the van merged onto the highway to Moscow. The four-lane highway was the main route from Moscow to St. Petersburg. The road was clogged with large commercial trucks and bumper to bumper traffic going both ways. Our van was not going anywhere fast. In my jetlagged haze I noticed that the bolder drivers, including our van driver, were using the shoulder as a third lane — a common practice, it worked until the shoulder ran out or there was a broken-down truck in the way, at which point everyone merged back into the proper lane.

Dark black smoke belched out of the exhaust pipes of the older trucks, and I realized that the air quality in this city of ten million was not going to be the same as the clean fresh air of Vancouver Island. Some of the trucks looked brand new (which they were) as the factory had not changed their design since the 1960's. The older vehicles crawled along looking like old cockroaches with legs missing. Tilting to the side they did not seem road worthy, and we saw many of them on the shoulder of the road with tires missing and axles broken.

As we crawled down the highway, we saw an impressive memorial statue located in the middle of a parking lot for a large mall. The Ezhe monument consisted of three oversized anti-tank devices which had been invented by Mikhail Gorikker to stop German tanks. The monument marked the exact spot where the German army had been halted during the Second World War. As we drove by, I was struck by how significant this war was to the Russians and it gave me a better understanding of the diplomatic tensions between the two countries.

******

When Michael and I arrived in Moscow we worried about the potential for difficulties with the police. The urban legend was that police officers commonly requested "fees" for imagined transgressions. The myth became a reality when one of our co-workers walking home from a restaurant was stopped by the police. When he could not produce his passport or any identification documents, he was put in the back of a police van and driven around the area. The police would not let him out of the van until he paid the appropriate "fine."

After hearing about this event Michael and I always carried our passports and embassy card with us. The embassy "get out of jail free card" clearly stated in English and Russian that we were Canadian citizens and technical diplomats of the Canadian embassy. There was a number to call, but our unfortunate friend did not have this card on him when the police asked for his identification.

******

Cars and driving

Michael's main focus during our first year in Moscow was to develop the middle school band program. He needed the flexibility of staying at the school after class in order to do this well. We were dependent on the school's shuttle bus service, which picked us up in the morning, but left the school at 4:00 pm. Returning home from the school using public transport was an issue. Our apartment was in the suburbs with no direct metro service. To get home we had to travel downtown and transfer at two busy metro stations to get onto the metro line that serviced our neighbourhood.

Many teachers at the school owned cars. A car increased the flexibility of getting to and from the school as well as traveling within the city on weekends. Options included diplomatic cars, which had been brought in across the border without paying tax. The downside to these cars was that they were subject to the import tax when decommissioned. Typically, diplomatic cars passed from teacher to teacher until they stopped working entirely, at which point the last owner paid the taxes owed. Available diplomatic cars tended to be older. Michael was reluctant to buy an old clunker that was going to require a lot of servicing.

Michael and I could not afford to buy a new car, so we bought a five-year-old Skoda Felicia from a school guard. The Skoda had been imported by a Russian company, and all the appropriate taxes had been paid. As we were employed as technical diplomats by the Canadian embassy, we had to register the car to receive embassy licence plates. These were always red.

To get its red licence plate we left the car at the Canadian Embassy for a few days. We were never told what they did to the car, but we were pretty sure the embassy staff placed a locator inside. Our suspicions were raised when the radio never worked properly after we picked the car up. The whole process was reversed when we sold the car five years later. The Canadian embassy took the car in for two days, removed the red plates, and the radio was back to normal. In addition, when we were driving to St. Petersburg the checkpoint guards did not seem at all surprised as we drove by. It was as though they were expecting us.

The red plates had a purpose as they identified the driver as being foreign and connected to a specific embassy. The first three numbers were based on when the country established diplomatic ties with the newly established Soviet Union. The UK's code was 001, Canada was 002 and the USA was 004. The middle school principal supplied a list of licence plate codes when we arrived, and Michael and I tried to remember the ones we saw the most.

There were definitely perks to having red technical diplomatic licence plates. Traffic police at intersections held batons that were striped black and white. The police would point at cars that had broken traffic laws and wave their striped sticks for them to pull over. These sticks were called *pozhaluysta* (if you please) sticks by the Russians. The police on the inner ring roads took their jobs seriously and the most common infractions were turning left and going through red lights. When the policemen saw the red plates, they usually waved the car on knowing that the driver probably did not speak Russian, understand the infraction, or know how to pay the penalty.

Michael was told by our local friends that when the police flagged them over for a minor traffic infraction, "bribery" had been successful in preventing official tickets. A few hundred rubles hidden inside the car documents usually ended with a polite warning. Luckily, Michael and I did not have to put this to the test. During the five years we drove in Moscow we were never "*pozhaluysta* sticked." I am certain that the red plates, and our apologetic looks, saved us from a few illegal left turn tickets.

In another instance, our car's red plates prevented our car from being towed away. One winter evening we had gone to the Canadian embassy. We had parked the car on the street with all the other cars. When we returned to the car it was sitting there all alone with no other cars in sight. This was highly unusual. We then saw signs that probably told us not to park after a certain time for snow removal. Thankfully the very efficient car towing enterprise, which we saw a block away removing parked cars, had deemed it unwise to tow the red plated car. Very lucky for us as we would not have known where the car had been towed to, and how to get it back.

******

Our trusty Skoda was a great car for Moscow driving. Not too big and not too small we blended in with the local driving community. The car came with four winter tires, which were to be put on when the snow fell in October. Snow tires or winter tires were made from a different type of rubber and had bigger treads than summer tires, so had more traction. In Winnipeg I used winter tires with steel studs sticking out of the rubber. The tires were removed in the spring once the roads were clear of ice. The Skoda's winter tires were not studded, but they had to be stored somewhere when they were not on the car. Like the rest of the residents of our building, Michael placed them on our balcony.

When Michael changed the tires the first winter it was not much fun. Changing four tires with emergency tire tools was a workout and frustrating when the bolts were partially seized. After living through the first winter of heavy snowfall, Michael and I realized that the streets were not as icy as those in central

Canada. The Moscow snow removing equipment was top notch. The use of a salt mixture allowed most of the streets to be ice free. The winter snow that fell on roads turned into a slushy wet mess, and we had to wash the car frequently. We decided that using all-season tires would be better than changing tires twice a year.

Our quest to find all-season radial tires was frustrating. We discovered that an item that was common in Canada was not always available in Russia. Michael asked a Russian speaking friend to phone tire shops to find all-season radials only to learn that the local mechanics did not have access to this "new" kind of tire. We then tried the high-end dealerships. After many disappointing calls we found one Audi service store that sold Pirelli tires. They had one set of all-season radials. The only four tires of this kind in Moscow they had been brought in for a display. After much intense discussion, the salesmen finally agreed to sell them to us.

His rationale was that if he sold us the tires, we would ruin the display. But as we now knew, the tires were only available in the display. Luckily for us the sale of the tires outweighed the aesthetic value of the display. In another situation, when we were looking for outdoor clothing, the salesperson refused to sell us a coat on display even though it was exactly what we needed. They were not allowed to sell anything on display as it was for advertising, even though the store did not sell any of the items within the display.

******

Our lovely Skoda had a sunroof that had been put in by the previous owner. A nice feature, but it started to leak. Beginning with a small drip it quickly became a waterfall directly onto my head. Our mechanic refused to get involved with something that had been put in by an amateur, so Michael bought some sealant and squirted it around the outside cracks of the sunroof. His solution worked for a while, but during the winter the sealant continually shrunk and expanded. The leak returned with a vengeance in the spring when the sunroof just did not close properly. It got so bad that we had to cover the car with a shower curtain when we parked to keep the rain out. In order to drive to work in the rain we set up wicks using strings inside the car, so the drips traveled away from our heads. We always kept dry towels in the back to be used when the seats got wet.

After numerous attempts to fix the leak, we decided to seal the window permanently closed using roofing tar. To prep the surfaces Michael used the cheapest bottle of Stolichnaya vodka he could find to remove all the old sealant and any remnant of caulking or foam. The vodka worked really well, and we have often recommended its use as an all-purpose cleaner. Michael put copious amounts of tar around the edges of the window and closed it as tightly as possible. He also put liberal amounts on the outside seams to make sure there were no cracks for water to get through. The roofing tar expanded and contracted with the temperature. Our unorthodox solution was a great success for the rest of the time we were in Russia.

******

Our international driver's licences were only valid for six months, so we got Russian drivers' licences. The Canadian Embassy human resource department supplied the necessary forms, which we filled out and returned to them. Next, we had to go to the licencing office located in the southeastern part of the city. Moscow traffic patterns were notoriously bad, and we were told to take a full day off work for this errand.

Michael and I arrived at the embassy in the morning and climbed into a van driven by Boris, "the embassy fixer," not knowing what to expect. He drove for about two hours through various neighborhoods. I noted that many of the buildings were from the Soviet era. The three-to-five story "Stalin" buildings had originally been built in the 1950's to address the housing crisis after the Second World War. I found out later that these buildings were called Khrushchyovka, and large groves of fruit and shade trees had been planted between them. They were prefab apartments designed only to last twenty-five years. Outdated and in poor repair they were in the process of being replaced by modern high rise apartment buildings, an initiative that had not reached this section of the city.

After close to two hours of driving, Boris turned into a gated building complex. We saw long lines of people standing outside in front of various doors. We had been told by colleagues that long line ups were common at government visa offices. A friend had spent hours in a line in order to get a Chinese visa for a holiday. While he waited, he had noticed that people would take turns standing and sitting in an organized way so that they would not lose their place in line. He even suspected that people were paid to stand in line to hold spots. Luckily, we were on embassy business. Boris took us to the back of the building where the special door reserved for diplomats was located.

We entered a long, dimly lit, empty corridor, typical of many Russian buildings. This spy movie cliché is founded on reality. The floor was covered in thick linoleum. The patterned material had been rolled out over door sills and other obstructions as if it were a carpet. Many buildings we entered in Russia had the same decor, both inside and out. Early on, our principal had commented that many apartment building exteriors looked like they had been finished with bathroom tiles.

Boris led us towards a door that was not marked with any sign, just a number. He told us to stand in the hallway while he went in. At this point Michael and I realized that we were at the mercy of Boris's good will. We had no idea where we were and what we would do if he decided to abandon us. Fortunately, he came out quickly enough and he led us into the room where a man was sitting behind Plexiglas.

Boris told us to show the man our Canadian drivers' licences and then sign our names in the places indicated on a form handed to us. We blindly trusted that we were signing driving license papers. As nothing else was required we returned to the van and drove back to the embassy. We had taken a day off work and driven for hours in order to sign our names on a form. Boris told us that our new driver's licences would be delivered to the embassy, and they would forward them to the school. My take-away from this experience was that getting government documents in Moscow involved long dark hallways and unmarked doors. Our status within the embassy made life much easier.

******

When Michael and I started driving in Moscow we were shocked and amazed by the different cars we saw. Expensive cars would weave between Ladas and Fords. Small convoys of black cars with blue lights traveling a meter apart would drive at excessive speeds in lanes designated for them. When the traffic volume increased drivers filled any space that became available, idiotically creating a situation where no one could move.

Parking on sidewalks was normal and we had to learn the rules used at various intersections. Cars exiting off large roads like Rublevskoye Shosse onto side-roads had the right of way over people driving on the side-road. The side roads had small signs at these special intersections. We had trouble interpreting them, but we watched and followed what the other drivers did. Cars would slow down and stop at the intersection if cars exited off the large road. If no one exited off the highway they did not stop. Driving through the intersection ourselves required nerves of steel and a lot of courage to trust that the cars would stop as we exited off Rublevskoye Shosse to get home.

Negotiating the roads of Moscow required a calm demeanor, defensive driving habits, and the ability to read the Russian alphabet. Very few signs were in English, so Michael and I purchased a map in Cyrillic. Using the Cyrillic map increased our ability to figure out where we were. We matched the letters on the map to the signs, and we were able to plan routes to various destinations and return home without difficulty. Finding street signs was challenging as they tended to be placed on the corner of buildings at different heights—a practice common in European cities.

Accidently Michael and I learned that the twelve-lane outer ring road called the MKAD was the city boundary. We crossed it one day when we became confused by the signs and missed our exit lane. After driving underneath the MKAD, we found ourselves on a two lane road in a dense forest. There were no houses to be seen, and both sides of the road were lined with ten-metre walls topped with razor wire. The sheer height of the walls was impressive and they went on for kilometres. When we finally found a place to turn around, we realized that the walls were the security perimeters for the mansions of the Russian oligarchs. The land would never be a part of any urban plan.

******

Moscow's road map looked like a bicycle wheel. The Kremlin was the hub in the center and major roads branched out from it like spokes. The larger spoke roads connected Moscow to the other major Russian cities like St. Petersburg. The MKAD was the final ring. Unmanned check point buildings and larger moveable barriers were located where the spoke roads crossed it. I imagined that the whole city would have been "locked down" within minutes when these building were staffed. Knowledge of this basic city plan, as well as our well-used map, helped us navigate to our favourite destinations in the days before global navigation systems were common.

There were four circle roads in the city. The first encircled the Kremlin complex and was the beginning point of the spokes. The second ring was called the Garden Ring or Boulevard Ring. It was well known for its traffic jams as well as the beauty of its boulevards. The boulevards had been lined with poplar trees commissioned by either Joseph Stalin or Nikita Khrushchev to beautify the city. The poplar tree had been chosen because it was fast growing, but the impact of its seed production had not been considered.

There were so many trees that at the height of the season the dandelion-like seeds or *pukh* would fall like a blizzard and the fluffy stuff would gather in piles. Teenagers lit these piles on fire for fun, and the flames would often travel many metres in the blink of an eye. Our allergy-suffering friends were not happy when *pukh* season started, and I shared my antihistamine supply with them. I found the two weeks of white fluffy seeds quite beautiful, and the majority of Muscovites loved the trees.

There was a third ring road, conveniently called the Third Ring. The six-lane road contained long tunnels that had been used in the car chase scenes of major action movies. The tunnels were an engineering challenge with underground exits going out and in as the road crossed the spoke roads and went under the main river. These tunnels were poorly engineered at the river crossings. It was common for water to seep in during the winter and freeze. Many traffic accidents occurred due to the icy conditions. Michael and I used a small part of this large circle road to get to our badminton lessons, but it was always a bit of a gamble due to accidents. We started using a longer, less busy route as it was not as likely to be plugged with cars and trucks.

The last ring road, the MKAD, completely circled the city. Michael and I took this route home from school a few times, but we discovered that daily traffic accidents and the sheer volume of cars and trucks made this route a nightmarish three-to-four-hour crawl home. The main cause of the congestion was the design of the overpass intersections. People exiting the MKAD had to merge with the traffic trying to enter the MKAD. This same small stretch of road was used by both groups and worked when the number of cars was small. Designed for a light traffic flow, the road became completely blocked when the number of cars increased.

After bad experiences with gridlock traffic, we only used the MKAD on the weekends before ten o'clock when the traffic was guaranteed to be light. Our usual destination was the IKEA Mega Mall located on the fourth spoke intersection going south. Getting to the Mall was quick, but returning after a few hours of shopping was unpredictable. Moscow traffic was so horrible that we never planned to do more than one thing in a day. We had to revise this habit when we returned to Canada.

Going to the Mega Mall and IKEA gave us a western retail experience as well as access to specific storage items for our apartment. Friends from our building would join us for these outings as IKEA meatballs satisfied their need for "Western" food. Michael and I enjoyed the coffee, as well as the smorgasbord line where we picked out what we wanted to eat rather than struggle with a menu. Typically, we would walk through the display corridors, stop for lunch, and then pick out our purchases before heading home.

Across the parking lot from IKEA was the French-owned mega food store Auchan. Bigger was better in Moscow, and there were 103 tills at the front. At least ninety internal aisles were filled with food products. Food items could be found in bulk proportions and shoppers filled their grocery carts to overflowing. When checking out, the line-ups per till were frequently ten people long. I even saw people reading books while they waited. Michael and I only went in a few times as the savings were not worth the long wait times.

The Mega Mall included a section filled with retail stores as well as an indoor skating rink, an IMAX theatre, large versions of electronic stores, and a Marks & Spencer. I never bought anything from any of the shops in the Mega Mall except Auchan and IKEA. The prices were higher than in Canada. Michael and I did not have a lot of extra money at this point in our international teaching careers.

******

Driving in Russia was entertaining as well as stressful. It was not uncommon to see cars backing up on roads, especially on highway exit ramps or after a major intersection. No one seemed to mind this unconventional behavior, and I empathized with the drivers. On a few occasions we missed our turn, which added close to an hour to our journey. There were very few places to turn around safely.

Crossing multiple lanes on the spur of the moment to buy flowers was common practice. Our usual route from downtown was to drive along Kutuzovsky Prospect for a few kilometres before exiting to merge onto Rublevskoye Shosse. These roads were three to five lane highways with a speed limit of 80 km/hr. Small kiosks sold flowers along the sides of these busy roads to service the businessmen driving home.

Flowers were a traditional gift for friends and family throughout the year for all kinds of occasions. In addition to birthdays and anniversaries, husbands gave flowers to their wives if they thought they were going to get in trouble for something. It was not uncommon for drivers going 80 km/hr to suddenly swerve across three lanes to stop in front of these small flower shops. At busy times cars were double parked, which caused the flow of traffic leaving town to slow and sometimes stop.

Adding to the entertainment of cars swerving for flowers were the "blue light" Audis. Cars with blue flashing lights placed on their roofs had privileges. Motorcades of black Audis with flashing lights would drive at breakneck speed down the designated lanes of Kutuzovsky Prospect literally a metre apart. When these convoys came up behind cars, the cars were expected to move out of the way immediately, regardless of how safe it was to do so. Members of parliament were given the blue lights as part of their service, but wealthy oligarchs also bought them.

In 2006 there was a protest related to an accident where a "blue light" passenger was killed when their driver turned left into oncoming traffic expecting them to stop. Originally the driver of the oncoming car was found at fault as he had not yielded to the "blue light" when it turned in front of him. Immediately afterward the decision, tens of thousands of Muscovites drove around the city with special ribbons on their antennae to show their displeasure. The ruling was reconsidered by the courts. As a result, the number of official "blue lights" distributed to the wealthy decreased. Fewer people used them because of the public outrage they received.

The traffic privileges of government officials did not stop at blue lights. Major roads like Kutuzovsky Prospect and Rublovskoye Shosse were frequently blocked off in the morning and evenings as high-ranking members of parliament traveled to work and back from their mansions located outside of town. Traffic congestion increased considerably at these times and impacted the lives of millions of commuters daily. The citizens of Moscow showed their displeasure with closures by posting the traffic jams caused by the stoppages on social media.

Our daily commute to school took about twenty minutes in the morning. We left early as the traffic was light, and occasionally saw the remains of car accidents that had occurred the night before. The most baffling was the Mercedes SUV overturned in the middle of the boulevard. We concluded excessive speeding was the most likely cause as the driver had to jump over concrete barriers to get where they landed.

Because of increased traffic in the afternoon, our return trip took at least an hour. One time the traffic was so congested we decided to stop going our usual route and drove all the way downtown and out again. The opening of a new bridge across the Moskva River during our last year decreased the afternoon travel time considerably. More importantly, our new route removed the need to make the "left turn of death" which was the climactic end of every school day.

The left turn was necessary to get to our building complex and it was not controlled by lights. The road we were trying to turn onto was four lanes. As it was the service road for Rublovskoye Shosse the traffic was usually heavy. We would join other cars waiting to turn left. As the number of cars increased the impatient drivers would pull up and line up in rows of two or even three waiting for an opportunity to turn left. Michael became very good at positioning himself with a "blocker" to his left so that when they went, we would follow beside them. Accidents at this intersection, preventable had there been traffic light, occurred on a weekly basis. We were fortunate never to be involved in any of them.

Defensive driving habits learned in Canada spared us from accidents though there were a lot of close calls. We had one minor fender bender, but luckily there was no damage to either car. As neither of us wanted the police involved Michael shook hands with the driver and we drove away. A few of our friends had more serious accidents caused by other drivers going through red lights. In most cases foreigners were automatically found at fault in car accidents. The rationale was that if the foreigner had not been there, there would not have been an accident. A space/time perspective that was convenient for the locals, and indefensible by the foreigner. We heard one story where a very honest Russian driver had to convince the policeman to assign blame to him and not the foreigner.

Cars were used to transport the strangest things. It was not unusual to see the back seats of cars packed full of watermelons and cucumbers. In some instances, goats and calves were put inside cars or on the back of small trucks. We were not sure where they came from or where they were going. There were no farms inside the MKAD. One day we saw a cheetah sticking its head out the window of a black Audi. Obviously the big cat was a pet, but it was still shocking for us to see a wild animal in a private car. After a few years of seeing everything and anything in the back of cars nothing surprised us.

******

When in Moscow we saw a unique strategy used when crews paved parking lots and sidewalks. The Russian method was simple. If there was something in the way the crew paved around or over it. Their method explained the half-submerged car tire embedded in the sidewalk just outside our apartment's gate. Rather than move the tire they had paved over it. We watched the same practice when they paved the parking lot of the building next door. All the cars had been moved but one. With all the machines in place, rather than stopping and waiting for the owner to show up, the team paved around the car.

******

Izmaylovo

A tourist destination, Izmaylovo market was a reconstructed walled town located within the historical park land of the Romanov noble family. The park also contained historical churches as well as the lake Peter the Great had sailed on as a boy. Inside the market were reconstructions of traditional buildings and rows and rows of kiosks selling Russian arts and crafts. Merchandise ranged from expensive jewelry, glassware, and wooden carvings to a flea market area where locals would sell their "treasures" from blankets on the ground. Izmaylovo was a very popular place, full of locals as well as foreign tourists brought by buses from the hotels. Everything you could think of buying could be found there.

Our first trip to Izmaylovo was during our orientation week for new teachers. It cost ten rubles or fifteen cents to get inside the gate. We were amazed by the size and diversity of the market. Expensive Persian carpets and hand painted wooden boxes were just up the crowded aisles from kiosks selling pirated DVDs. On our first trip we barely scratched the surface of the huge complex.

We quickly organized a second trip with our new friends Karen and Mark. They had the same passion for local crafts and DVDs.

On the way to Izmaylovo it was easy to miss the right turn off the Garden Ring Road. The road entrance looked more like a parking lot than a street. Whoever was navigating really had to pay attention. A missed turn meant that we had to drive to the next overpass, do a U-turn and then, as there was no left turn allowed, a second U-turn was necessary at the next bridge overpass, at which point we were ready to attempt the right turn on the road to Izmaylovo again. All the extra driving added half an hour to the trip, more if the Ring Road was busy.

After we gained confidence reading the Moscow street map, and negotiating the various turns, Michael and I drove to Izmaylovo frequently with friends in tow. Our main goal was to find new movies and have lunch at the shashlik kiosk. Shashlik was a meat dish where skewers of pieces of lamb, pork or beef marinated in spices, were cooked over hot coals. We soon added Russian words for chicken, pork, and lamb to our vocabulary so we could order the variety of shashlik we wanted.

After eating I enjoyed walking around the stalls looking at the beautiful arts and crafts. Many people were employed by factories to produce traditional folk art. Certain cities produced painted lacquered boxes while others focused on small wooden boxes made from birch bark. Crystal glassware, blue porcelain, and lace linens were other common traditional items with strong folk-art roots. The most popular wooden products for tourists were carved Santa Clauses and traditional Russian nesting dolls.

Over the five years we went there, the Izmaylovo market changed. A large section of tents that sold leather goods existed outside the walls in 2004, but it had disappeared by 2008. The actual number of cheap clothing and handbag kiosks in front of the main gate decreased significantly as the government cracked down on illegal imports. On the positive side, more parking lots were built, and the reconstructions of a palace and church were completed and opened as museums.

The first kiosks within the complex were small tents filled with mass produced items. Black market movies and music as well as cheap tourist napkins and aprons were sold here. The more permanent artisans were located past the tents in wooden buildings specifically designed to show their wares—hand-painted wooden objects such as traditional nesting dolls and birch bark items. Izmaylovo was a maze, but arts and crafts were set up in specific areas. For instance, paintings and etchings were sold along a tree lined pathway just past the carpet selling area.

Smoke and the aroma of cooked meat assaulted everyone as they walked through the entrance gate. A number of *shashlik* restaurants were located along the wall to the right. At the kiosks skewers of meat were hand-turned on waist high open-air bar-becues. The vendors only took cash, and the deliciously cooked meat was served on a paper plate beside a piece of rye bread. A garnish of pickles and onions completed the meal. Beverage choices included beer, tea, or soda.

People sat in wooden booths opposite the barbecues. The bench seats were not comfortable. The other option was to climb a flight of stairs to a second floor above the fires. Here there were comfortable plastic chairs, but smoke from the barbecues down-stairs would drift up the stairs and fill the room. In the summer we sat at the outside tables. In the winter, when the temperature was minus five or lower the warmer upstairs room was the more attractive option even though the health of our lungs suffered.

Another eatery at Izmaylovo was located behind the tents on the left. This restaurant catered to the workers at the market and served two items — a large caldron of lamb pilaf and a large pot of traditional borscht accompanied by rye bread. Michael and I had noticed the kiosk on one of our first trips, but chose not to try it even though it looked and smelled good. At the time we were not sure that the food preparation methods met the hygiene standards that we were used to in the west. We did not wish to risk food poisoning. We had heard many horror stories from friends.

As the years passed the price of shashlik increased and the portion size decreased. We reconsidered trying the pilaf kiosk. Michael and I thought that it would not be in the best interest of the pilaf vendor to poison their local customers so it would probably be safe. We ordered the rice pilaf — a mixture of vegetables, rice and lamb served with the mandatory pickle. The only beverage offered was beer. As it was winter, the owner encouraged us to eat inside a plastic tent at plastic picnic tables. We ate our bowls of steaming pilaf and drank our beer while fully dressed in our winter clothes. Inside the tent it was a few degrees warmer than the outside, minus 20°C. Despite the temperature, the pilaf was delicious, and the meal was only a few dollars for both of us compared to the twenty dollar shashlik meals. We continued to go there for lunch when we traveled to Izmaylovo.

The most satisfying finds at Izmaylovo we discovered in the areas located at the edges of the complex at the back or up the steps away from the initial kiosks. The more remote areas were where the actual artists set up their stalls. When I bought something from them, I knew I was supporting their families directly.

Over the years we spent in Russia we returned to the same artisan booths at Izmaylovo. The artists were always happy to see us, and we would try to converse in our limited Russian. Michael and I left Moscow with well over fifty small carved boxes and wooden figures. My favourites, a small carved and painted cat, a ceramic fish, as well as wooden kitchen good luck charms, traveled to all our subsequent jobs in my hand luggage.

******

26 Rublevskoye

For four years Michael and I lived in an apartment complex at 26 Rublevskoye Shosse. Located in the northwest part of Moscow close to the Krylatskoye rowing canals built for the 1980 Summer Olympics, Rublevskoye was one of three complexes used by the school to house teachers. These buildings were controlled by the Russian government and housed embassy employees as well as smaller embassies. The three apartment complexes were surrounded by chain linked fencing and had twenty-four-hour security guards at the gate. The other two housing locations were downtown. We chose to live in one called Gruzinski for our last year to be closer to our friends who lived there.

The three apartment buildings at Rublevskoye were seventeen floors high and positioned to create a semi-circle around a playground. The nine entrances had elevators, which serviced two apartments on each floor. We lived at entrance nine. During the first weeks of school a fellow teacher asked us to join him, and some of the other teachers who lived in the buildings, for refreshments in the play area. In the recent past people had not been allowed to gather in large groups in public. Penalties included being arrested and fined, so we kept one eye out for the guards, ready to throw everything into the back of the car if they appeared. Thankfully the guards were not interested in us and we were able to relax and get to know each other better.

Our apartment was approximately one hundred square metres. We found out later that it was two standard Russian apartments converted into one. The schools' embassies had insisted that North American and British employees required more space than Eastern Europeans. The apartments were maintained and furnished by Olga and her crew of "green guys." The "green guys" were so named because they wore green uniforms. They were handymen who could fix anything that might go wrong within an apartment. To create equity and decrease complaints the school furnished all the apartments the same including the plates, dishes, and other basic kitchen utensils.

The views from our fifteenth-floor apartment looked out onto the Moskva River and the parks that ran on either side of it. The Stalin era "Seven Sisters" buildings, located in the distant downtown, could be seen when the sun shone off their sandstone surfaces. The number of trees and parks was a pleasant surprise. The parks provided places to relax and enjoy nature. Fruit trees, planted decades earlier by the residents, produced bountiful crops available to anyone who wanted them.

A large park with a small historic church perched on the top of a hill was accessible across the dual carriageway beside our apartment. The church was known for its healing spring, which bubbled up from an aquafer. We recommended the park when my parents came to visit in 2005. My mother loved the area so much that she returned the next day to paint the church, as well as the people gathering water from the spring.

******

Our apartment was a twenty-minute walk from the newly opened RAM Store. This small supermarket chain sold household goods as well as food. One day as we walked home, we witnessed an altercation between a pair of men and a third man in a car. The argument started with yelling, which was then followed by the two men punching the third. The people on the sidewalk kept walking, eyes carefully averted, and we did the same. The yelling stopped when a "Baba" (Russian grandmother) walked towards the two men wagging her finger, obviously telling them to behave. One of the men stopped his attack long enough to shrug his shoulders and verbally defend himself, as if to say, "What? He needed to be beaten." When we heard the sirens of the police, we quickened our pace and left the area.

******

The closest metro station to where we lived was called Molodezhnaya. The station was a fifteen-minute walk from our apartment and the ride downtown took about half an hour. The Molodezhnaya line ran above ground most of the way. It was nice to watch the city go by before going below ground level. The station by the Kremlin was called Aleksandrovskiy Sad, and we would get off there to walk to all the historic buildings in the downtown area.

Just outside the entrance to the Molodezhnaya metro station was a building with a small Cyrillic sign, which said *producti*. The word translated to "products." Inside we found a large open space filled with kiosks containing fruits, vegetables, meat, cheese, and other household products. These markets were found in every neighbourhood. They ranged in size from small convenience stores to large open format markets. The Molodezhnaya *producti* was large and always busy with locals buying groceries as they returned home from work.

Michael and I were happy to have found a place to buy fresh vegetables and fruit, but initially we found it daunting. No one spoke English. We had to communicate using our English-Russian dictionary and mime. We copied the behaviours of the locals, brought our own bags and waited in orderly lines to be served. Michael was able to pronounce Russian words easier than me, so he did most of the ordering.

The central area of the market building was devoted to the butchers who cut raw meat on large wooden cutting blocks. The blocks were well worn and did not look too clean to our western eyes. The heads of sheep and goats were laid out for sale along with their organs. In addition, there were various cuts that I had trouble recognizing and refrigeration did not seem to be important. We bought our pork tenderloins from the few stalls that had freezers and refrigerators.

We bought a fresh leg of lamb once. The leg was attached to the shoulder, but we managed to communicate that we wanted only the leg. The vendor pulled out a hatchet and proceeded to chop his way through the joint. Although the lamb was tasty, we spent a significant amount of time digging out bone chips created by the hatchet. We did not buy lamb from that butcher again.

Even though the rows of booths sold the same produce, we returned to the same helpful and friendly vendors. Michael and I had our favourite fruit and vegetable lady, our favourite cheese stall, and our favourite spice and nut seller. The spice seller did not speak English, but he could sing a Frank Sinatra song "New York, New York." He would start singing as soon as he saw us and everyone in the building knew that the foreigners had arrived.

Shopping at the *producti* became a weekly event. The sellers started to recognize us and they practiced English words while we practiced our Russian. They never took advantage of our ignorance of the Russian language. When we mistakenly gave them too much money they would smile, take what they needed, and hand the rest back.

One time we saw two horses tied to a post outside the *producti*. There were horse stables located a few kilometres down the main road by the river. The horses had been ridden up from the paddocks and their owners were inside. It was an unexpected sight, and we took pictures to document the event. Where else would you find riding horses tied up outside a food store in a city the size of Moscow?

******

Inside the *producti* I tried different Russian cheeses. There was a popular smoked cheese, which pulled apart like string. I learnt how to order *tvorog*, a young cheese used to make a pancake called *syrniki*. One time we bought a Russian sour cream, thinking it was yogurt. The hard cheeses were easier, but the selection was not predictable and the variety was nothing like we found in Europe. Whenever she travelled, a friend would always bring cheese back in her suitcase.

Michael and I made some mistakes when we bought food at grocery stores because we could not read the labels and the pictures were not always accurate. Other than the presence of aisles of alcohol the grocery stores were set up like the typical Canadian supermarket. We picked our groceries from the shelves and paid at the front till. One day we decided to try a tube of what we thought was liverwurst. The checkout lady tried to tell us in Russian what it was—she could tell we did not know, but we bought it anyway. To our horror it turned out to be a tube of white fat.

******

One day we took our friend Kate to the *producti* market. The nut and spice guy was happy to see us and mimed that we should follow him out of the building. His behaviour was unusual, but he was very insistent. The other vendors nodded their heads in support of our going with him. I could not think of any reason why we should not follow him, so we did.

We walked down the street for a few blocks. I was having doubts, but when we turned the corner into an alley, we saw a group of people gathered in the space behind a building. There was a barbecue and skewers of meat were being cooked over an open fire. Plates and utensils sat on a covered table beside sliced rye bread and salad greens. After miming and trying our sparse Russian vocabulary we discovered that it was our vendor's birthday. The fact that he had invited us indicated that he considered us as part of his family.

Michael, Kate and I accepted food and drinks from these friendly strangers and joined the party. It was a "Moscow moment" that none of us has forgotten. The generosity of the nut man to include us in a family celebration was completely unexpected and the memory continues to bring a smile to my face.

We were told that Russians were stereotypically stoic and unfriendly. When we asked our Russian friends about this reputation, they told us that they did not understand why you would smile at a stranger. Being smiled at was suspicious and made no sense if you did not know the person. Once the vendors saw us a few times at the *producti* and *Gorbushka* they were always friendly and helpful.

Over time the development of large supermarkets had a negative impact on the smaller local markets. Ramstore was the first international food chain to open. Seven Continents and Auchan quickly followed. Metro and other discount box stores became as popular in Moscow as in Europe and North America. The original local market at Molodezhnaya closed and was remodelled to meet the changes in consumer demand. The fruit, nut and vegetable vendors that we knew so well did not return.

******

After Michael and I became familiar with the metro and road systems we started to explore more of the city. Our Cyrillic map made it easier to match our location with the street signs. There were few bilingual signs because only a small number of foreigners lived in Moscow and few owned cars. The only places we saw English on signs were the tourist areas downtown.

When we ventured into non-tourist areas people were surprised and dismayed when they discovered we could not speak Russian. They were dismayed they could not help us with directions or information. Sometimes we reverted to pointing at the words in our Russian-English dictionary to communicate our destination. Translation apps have made traveling much easier.

In the early 2000s only a few could understand our attempts at speaking Russian. It might have been because they had never heard a foreigner attempt to speak Russian. We had difficulty with both the sounds and cadence of syllables.

Michael would attempt to speak Russian at restaurants and shops, but often it would take the server a few minutes to figure out that the words were Russian and not another language altogether. Conversely, Michael and I grew up hearing English words spoken and pronounced in many ways by immigrants from all over the world who made Canada their home. We were pretty good at gleaning meaning from context and physical gestures.

******

Our friend Jenni found an amazing Georgian restaurant as she was walking in our Rublevskoye neighbourhood. She was stopped by a woman handing out samples of Georgian bread on the street. Jenni did not understand much of what the woman was saying. She deduced that a new restaurant had opened, and she was being invited to attend that evening.

When Jenni told us about her experience we decided to go to the restaurant together. The proprietors were very excited to see us. Armed with our phrase book and limited Russian we managed to order lamb shashlik, cheese bread, walnuts, cheese wrapped in eggplant, as well as a salad plate. We were so impressed with the food we asked if we could take a menu to get translated. They refused, but the next time we went they gave us a newly translated English menu. There were some funny literal translations and usual grammar mistakes, but it was a great gesture.

The restaurant's name in English was "The Two Jugs", which referred to containers of oil or wine. The owners had decorated the interior in a pseudo-Mediterranean theme with plastic vines and paintings of grapes and landscapes on the walls. It was not uncommon for restaurants to have "themes" and this one was definitely Georgian with a twist. A large TV screen at one end of the room showed the equivalent of MTV videos, but the sound was turned off. In its place the restaurant played loud rock music from a Russian radio station. The picture and the sound never matched.

About a year after it opened the owners hired a karaoke singer. The singer started at seven o'clock, at which point the music volume would be turned up. At around eight o'clock large family groups would come to eat and enjoy the live music. In a celebratory mood, they would often get up and dance. Between karaoke sets, the background music would be put back on full blast, often with rap, which was punctuated with the usual expletives. Needless to say, we quickly learned to arrive early and leave before the entertainment started if we wanted to have conversations that did not require yelling.

******

Gorbushka

Prior to 1990 black market goods were imported illegally and sold at kiosks around the city. These products included anything that was not available in Russia. With the opening up of Russia to western capitalism the illegal business operations were legalized and became extremely lucrative. We heard of one example regarding toasters. Maintaining a firm grasp of the supply chain through political connections, the man who originally smuggled toasters into Russia became the only man allowed to legally import toasters. He quickly became an oligarch.

The open-air black-market stalls that sold software, videos, and electronics had been located in the city square by the Gorbunov Place of Culture. Called the "Gorbushka, the illegal kiosks were closed by the government in 2001 and relocated into the new Gorbushka dvor complex. Because of its size, Gorbushka dvor was a challenge to navigate. A city block of old warehouses had been renovated and joined together. Corridors and floor levels did not always match, and public bathrooms were difficult to find. The toilets were the typical squat style with no toilet paper provided.

When looking for bathrooms it was common to find squat toilets in various states of cleanliness. Moscow taught me never to venture out without a tissue packet in my pocket — I needed to be prepared for some awful bathroom experiences. My habit of carrying tissue continued in Bangladesh, Thailand, and the UAE, but was not as vital in Korea as Jeju had well serviced public bathrooms, cleaned and regularly stocked with toilet paper.

The first time Michael and I went into Gorbushka we were amazed at the sheer size of the complex. It was new and glitzy on the inside, which contrasted with its 1970 façade. As we explored, we found that the second floor of the second building had multiple rows of CD and DVD kiosks. Each space was labeled with a letter and number code, as well as an official looking document to highlight that they were legitimate. The remaining areas of Gorbushka were a maze of licensed retail outlets that sold computers, electronics, washing machines, and other household appliances. Gorbushka was the place to go to buy anything connected to technology and electricity.

Signs on a few booths advertised English movies, but buying pirated movies was a bit of a gamble. We learned to ask the vendor to play bits of the movie to make sure that the sound worked and the picture was relatively clear. Once we found a reliable source we returned when new releases came out. Acquiring movies from the Gorbushka was more convenient than traveling to Izmaylovo—we went there regularly.

When the USA film industry clamped down on pirating in the western world it affected the availability of English movies at Gorbushka and Izmaylovo. With the shortage of pirated DVDs, we were forced to download movies from the internet. Michael used Bit-torrent to provide us with English medium movies for the remainder of our overseas adventures. The availability of Netflix and other legal streaming systems removed the need to download entertainment illegally.

******

A block down the street from the Gorbushka was the entrance to a large open-air market. One day we decided to check it out. Inside we found rows of covered aisles with small shops selling clothing and household items. This outdoor version of a department store was very busy with locals doing their weekly shopping.

Fresh fruit and vegetables stalls were located at the back as well as aisles for cheeses and fresh meat displayed in refrigerators. Prices were cheaper than in supermarkets and the vendors were happy to tolerate our terrible Russian. When the *producti* by Molodezhnaya closed for renovations, we drove to the Gorbushka market for most of our groceries.

One day we saw what we thought was bacon in the butcher shop window. We had discovered that the bacon we were used to was not easy to find. Surprisingly there are numerous ways to cure pork belly and the western method was not universal. The butcher had many versions of pork belly and Michael and I tried all of them before settling on a smoked one that was the saltiest. Over the years we bought sausages and other interesting smoked meats which tasted like ham, but weren't necessarily pork.

The butcher's was a busy shop with a long line up. We gave our order quickly in our broken Russian, aided by our phrase book and fingers pointing. The lady who worked the counter got to know us and she would greet us with a big smile. On one occasion I thought I saw duck breasts at the back of the shop. Michael was getting pretty good at speaking Russian words with a reasonable accent. We had successfully ordered our bacon and sausages and using our pocket Russian dictionary we asked if what I saw was indeed duck. After looking at the translation in the book she nodded, but called them something that did not really match the words in the book. Michael asked her to repeat the words so that he could remember them for the next time.

Michael thought he had mastered the phrase as he used it over the next few months and the duck breasts appeared. One day there was a new person at the front and when Michael asked for duck, she was very confused. We were at a loss as to what to do until we heard our regular lady speak in Russian from the back of the shop. She said, "He doesn't speak Russian, but he wants...." and said a phrase which was not the same as the one that Michael had been using.

We asked a Russian friend what Michael had really been saying and he told us that he had been asking for "wild breasts." The first vendor had always accepted Michael's attempt—she knew what we wanted. Her response showed how accommodating the locals could be towards foreigners.

Our other favourite shop at the Gorbushka market was the bread kiosk. It sold fresh cheese bread called *khachapuri* as well as the Georgian variation of samosas. The meat filled bread pockets were tasty, well worth having to spit out the occasional piece of gristle. Their cheese breads were always baked fresh and sometimes we had to wait for a new batch to be ready. We both ate one immediately and took three or four home for later. Georgian cheese bread froze well, and we warmed them up in a frying pan to eat as a snack at the end of the workday.

******

We took our teacher friends to the Gorbushka market. These trips got us out of our "expat" bubble and into the everyday world of Moscow. Gorbushka revealed aspects of Russian life, from the wealthy in expensive suits buying apples to the poor pensioners who sold hand-knit items and vegetables on the sidewalk.

******

Signage and supply

In 2004 there were very few signs or advertising on the outside of buildings. Within complexes there were multiple entrances to different shops. If we did not have the exact entrance number the lack of window displays and store signs made it hard to know which door to open. Michael needed a piece of electronic equipment fixed and he got the address of a repair shop from a colleague. We found the building, but there was no signage at all and Michael did not see an obvious way to open the door. He finally noticed a small call button beside the door which he pushed. The door unlocked and he entered a fully functional electronics repair shop. I had opted to sit in the car and was a bit apprehensive about the fact that Michael had just disappeared through an unmarked door. I was relieved to see him re-emerge half an hour later.

My teaching friend, Bob, and I had a similar experience when we went looking for Volvo parts. We needed wiper blades and had been given the address by a reliable source. We found the building, but it looked completely abandoned. The sidewalks were overgrown and there was no evidence of any businesses. We walked around the building a few times looking at the doors and surroundings for anything that might suggest a car part shop. Finally, we spotted a sign on the ground. We turned it over to see the Volvo icon. Encouraged, we walked to the closest unmarked door and rang the bell. We were buzzed into a shop with all the Volvo parts imaginable. There were catalogues, places to sit, and the salesmen offered us drinks of tea or instant coffee. We soon departed with the windshield wiper blades that Bob needed.

Over the five years we were in Moscow, the uncertainty of not knowing what was behind doors changed. As more visitors arrived in the city, stores began to include window displays.

Along the Old Arbat it became easy to see which shops sold traditional arts and crafts and which ones sold clothing. Large new shopping malls opened downtown as well as in the suburbs. Window displays became the norm. As the economy grew Michael and I found pretty much anything that we wished for, including good coffee beans.

When we arrived in Moscow purchasing appliances was a complicated and time-consuming experience. Purchasing a toaster was an adventure. We went to a specialized kitchen store where we were the only customers. After looking at the options and deciding which toaster we wanted, Michael and I then spent ten minutes walking up and down aisles to find a salesperson. When we found a salesperson, he seemed reluctant to serve us. We insisted that we wanted to buy the toaster, so he finally wrote the item number down and looked it up on the computer. The toaster was in stock, and he filled out a form which we then took to the cashier. The cashier took our money and stamped three receipts with three different stamps. The cashier kept one receipt, gave us the remaining two, and sent us off to the "pick-up" counter. At this point we wondered if we had just been ripped off. However, the man behind the desk took his copy of the receipt and ran off to the back room.

On returning with the toaster in its box he unpacked it and plugged it in to see if it worked. This was the customary practice when buying electronics. It was better to make sure that whatever you were buying worked. If we took it home and it didn't work, it would not be replaced. After passing its inspection the toaster was repacked in its box and given to us.

******

In 2004 we could not find coffee beans in any of the shops in Moscow. The Russians drank instant coffee and the switch to drinking brewed coffee made with good quality beans would not happen for a few years. Both Michael and I were coffee drinkers and instant coffee was not an option. To remedy this problem my sister bought large bags of Starbucks coffee at Costco and mailed them to us via the embassy in Ottawa. In Ottawa the package was placed in the diplomatic pouch and flown across the planet to be delivered to us at our school. We felt a little guilty about the carbon footprint of our coffee habit, but not so guilty that we stopped drinking coffee. To supplement my sister's supply, we would buy coffee beans when we traveled to Europe and Canada, and carried them back in our suitcases. In our last year a Starbucks opened nearby and we were finally able to buy beans locally.

******

Socializing – restaurants and school events

International schools usually organized social events for their teaching staff as a team building strategy. At the beginning of each school year, the Anglo-American School encouraged everyone to attend staff barbecue dinners at the American dacha. The American Embassy had been awarded the privilege of using this government owned cottage complex during the Cold War. This dacha was located in the middle of the summer houses used by the rich oligarchs and politicians.

Surrounded by eight-foot walls the dacha included a large house that could sleep ten or more, a tennis court that had seen better days, as well as some ancient looking playground equipment. The American dacha was used all year round to stage events including birthday parties and winter ski parties.

Michael and I attended the annual staff parties and a few private birthday parties. At staff parties the large outdoor barbecues were used to cook pork shashlik, hotdogs, and burgers for over one hundred teachers and support staff. The amount of food was always sufficient, but the quality worsened as the years went by. In addition, the amount of free alcohol noticeably decreased. Even so, everyone enjoyed the beginning of the year dacha "retreat." It was a great way to reconnect with returning staff members and meet the newly hired teachers or "newbies."

Christmas staff events included dinners at ballrooms or other venues large enough to seat everyone. Michael and I would dress up in our finest and either drive or take the metro to the location. The weather was unpredictable and could vary from hovering around zero degrees to minus twenty degrees Celsius. On the metro it was common to see men and women dressed in fur coats and hats, obviously on their way to the opera or the theatre.

The first Christmas party we attended was held at the American ambassador's residence, a beautiful historic building built in the 18th century. It was a mansion with tall ceilings and period wallpaper and furniture. The event was a lavish affair with speakers and a full sit-down dinner with dancing afterward. Unfortunately, some teachers got a little too adventurous and strayed into areas that were off limits. Due to this bad behaviour, the school had to find an alternative venue the following year. As with the fall barbecues the Christmas parties decreased in splendor as time went on. The last one we attended only had finger-food tables and nowhere to sit or put our plates. The alcohol ran out before we had a chance to get our first drink, so we left.

At the end of the year each section of the school organized a dinner event to say goodbye to the teachers who had chosen to move on to different international schools or return home. The dinners were well attended, and speeches were made to departing colleagues. Michael and I joined our colleagues at a European-Swedish restaurant called Scandinavia. Seating areas in Scandinavia included a summer terrace deck area on the roof and a "beer garden" at the entrance. Because we were a large group we were given a set menu of hamburgers and a salad.

Scandinavia was located near Patriarch Pond, a historic park the size of a city block with a large pond in the center. The area around Patriarch Pond was a popular location for the wealthy elite and just down the street was another memorable restaurant called Café Margarita. Café Margarita was tiny and it was necessary to reserve a table in advance. The food was excellent. While we ate, we were entertained by live musicians playing classical and jazz music. The café and Pond were mentioned in the book *Masters of Margarita* written by Mikhail Bulgakov. People would walk around the blocks to get the essence of the place.

******

Our friends Karen and Mark took us to a Chinese restaurant that was tucked under an overpass along the ring road. As usual it was a challenge to find a place to park. The restaurant was in the basement of the building and had no natural light. When the waitress came, Karen asked for an English menu. It was common for restaurants to have a few menus translated into English. As we looked at the names of the dishes we started to chuckle. The translation errors could only have been made if the menu had been translated from Chinese into Russian, and then into English. Because there were no pictures, each order came as a complete surprise. "Mussels with spicy bean sauce" was pretty straight forward, but "soup of the green stuff" could have been anything, so we did not choose it. "Stewed froggy paws 'three glasses' in the Taiwan style" was also a mystery. What exactly were the "three glasses"? And, more importantly, I wasn't aware that frogs had paws. I ordered "fried chicken sternum with the lemon flavour" hoping it would be chicken breast. Chicken thighs appeared in a lovely sauce.

******

When eating out it was not uncommon for your dishes to appear in an order that did not necessarily make sense. My friend Toni remembers eating her dessert before the main meal arrived. She speculated that the cooks were making the main course from scratch and trying to keep her happy with something to eat. The larger the group the less likely it was that your food would come at the same time. We got used to eating when the food appeared and did not wait for our friend's plates.

One of the longest meals I ever experienced occurred at an Italian restaurant. There were six of us so we ordered pizza rather than pasta thinking it would be faster. When our pizzas were presented one at a time it became rather funny. As we paid, the waiter apologized for the waiting time and told us that their second oven had broken. Asking us to order a pasta dish rather than pizza had not crossed their minds. It was a "Moscow moment."

Michael and I witnessed the habit of businessmen finalizing deals in restaurants. Because of the uncertainty of the banking system many transactions were cash only. Negotiated deals included the handing over of satchels of money, handshakes, and large quantities of alcohol. At our first "Gala Ball", a yearly event organized to raise money for after school programs, we witnessed a man pulling bundles of cash from under the table contained in a sports bag. Bodyguards and tight security made sure that there were no issues with carrying that much cash to an event. The best moment of the evening was when they auctioned a dinner with the American ambassador which went for $20,000.00 USD. No problem: out came the sports bag and the required amount was counted out.

Michael and I acquired a fondness for eggs Benedict when we lived in Victoria, Canada while completing our master's degrees. There was a restaurant in the downtown core that was dedicated to breakfasts of all kinds. There were many varieties of eggs Benedict to choose from and they were all fabulous. We made a point of having breakfast there whenever we returned to Victoria. While overseas we searched to find eggs Benedict that matched the ones in Canada, but we were never successful. The ingredients were never the same, but the Pushkin Café in Moscow came close.

The interior décor of the Pushkin Café resembled the libraries of nineteenth century Russian nobility and the restaurant was named after the famous Russian poet and author, Alexander Pushkin. He, along with the rest of Russian high society, used to stroll along Tverskoy Boulevard in the late 1700s and early 1800s. Pushkin's family estate near Pskov was one of the highlights of the grade-six field trip, and I visited it five times. The scenic property had a lake with lilac trees lining the roads to the house. I can understand why Pushkin was inspired to write a novel while in exile as there was not much else to do. The closest town was a day's walk away.

The Pushkin café was very popular. It was easy for us to choose what we wanted to eat—they had English menus and English-speaking waiters. Michael and I enjoyed the ambiance and service levels of this restaurant. They even had a special stool for women's purses.

A specialty at the Pushkin Cafe was hot chocolate. In my experience hot chocolate was made of hot milk with one teaspoon of cocoa and sugar. In Russia, hot chocolate was made with a melted chocolate bar. It was a challenge to finish your teacup full of melted chocolate, but the object was to savor it slowly, over time.

Michael and I had some memorable experiences eating at high end restaurants. The "Two Barrels" (*Dve Bochka*) was an example of a theme restaurant popular with the Russian elite. Our friend, who worked in the oil industry, had gone there for a business lunch. He told us that the food was fantastic and that the atmosphere was worth experiencing. Even though we knew it was going to be at least one hundred dollars each I agreed to go to celebrate our birthdays. Dressed in our best outfits we parked our old Skoda Felicia around the corner so as not to get trapped by black Audi's that were always double parked in front of the restaurant.

The Two Barrel's featured a rustic carnivore theme. The décor was dark with brick walls and wooden beams. The room reminded me of a French chalet or medieval inn. The tables and chairs were solid wood and finished to look old. In the middle of the restaurant a whole pig was roasting on a spit over an open fire. I had never seen this before or since though I have eaten goats and pigs that have been cooked over open fires outside.

Their menu consisted of a selection of roasted meats served with side dishes. Michael and I had been unsuccessful when buying steaks at the butchers or in any other restaurant. The meat was not aged the way we were used to and they were always tough. We enjoyed a top-quality steak prepared by a first-rate chef. Michael ordered a steak slow cooked between two water-soaked birch logs. I chose a traditional tenderloin steak. Everything was cooked to perfection and the quality of the meat was outstanding. Good wine flowed freely. We returned to the Two Barrels for a farewell dinner for our friends, Kate and Kerry, who were leaving Moscow to start new jobs in an international school in Zambia.

******

Michael and I noticed that waiters tried their best not to offend or embarrass us. One of the first times we ventured outside of Moscow, we went to an old sanatorium that had been converted to a park. We decided to eat at the restaurant in the complex before heading home. There was an impressive looking menu with selections ranging from salads to steak dinners. Pictures on the menu made it easier to decide what to order.

We signaled the waiter to take our order and were a bit taken aback when he informed us that our selections were not available. We thought this was odd and asked for another few minutes to make a different choice. When he returned, he told us our new choices were also not available. Perplexed, we wondered why the kitchen did not have the food advertised on the menu. Michael had an idea. He asked what they had to eat. At which point the waiter breathed a sigh of relief and told us they had soups and rye bread. Michael and I laughed and ordered borsch.

The acceptance of the unexpected when ordering food was a sign of a well-seasoned expatriate. One time, Michael questioned what was brought out of the kitchen. The server got quite offended. He said, "This is what you ordered," which might indeed have been the case due to the language barrier. Michael and I became more understanding of the servers who had to deal with customers who did not speak their language and were busy pointing at pictures on the menu and holding up fingers for quantities. We ate many things that we were not expecting—unusual parts of a sheep as well as live abalone and sea snails.

******

Moscow Metro

The Moscow metro system transported millions of people every day. Traveling by metro was affordable as five tickets were less than a dollar. "*Pyat*" (five) was one of my first Russian words. People could travel on trains all day long if they did not exit the system. Homeless people rode the metro to keep warm. They were a common sight on the downtown brown circle line in the winter. The older metro cars had well-worn comfortable leather seats lining the walls and lots of space to stand. Newer cars were not as comfortable. They had plastic molded seats and were noisy. The doors made a horrible squealing sound when they opened and closed.

Once Michael and I recognized the signs leading to the metro stations, the entrances were easy to find. The metro system itself was huge with multiple lines. Each one was coded with both a color and number. Connections were well marked within the stations and even though the metro signs were written in Cyrillic we were able to match the station names to our map. Once we were orientated, we just followed the colored tiles to transfer to the next line. Individual stations were announced on an overhead PA system and the automated message directed passengers to the side the doors opened.

Moscow metro stations were aesthetically beautiful. The older stations of the brown line were full of historical art and frescos that promoted the propaganda of the time they were built. The newer stations continued the trend with incredible glitz and splendor reflecting the economic growth of the 2000s. Michael and I tried to go to as many of the stations as possible to see the works of art. In all my travels I have not seen anything that rivals the grandeur of the metro stations of Moscow.

To accommodate the fact that millions of people used the metro, the city planners built tunnels called *perekhod* at intersections as well as at other strategic places where people needed to cross multilane roads and highways. Depending on the size of the intersection and how many metro stations were nearby, *perekhods* could be complex mazes lined with shops and food vendors servicing commuters.

Stairways going into *perekhod* were quite steep. There were special rails designed for the wheels of baby carriages and bicycles on the steps, usually on the side or up the middle of the staircases. When my sister visited in 2006, she thought this innovation was brilliant. On a trip to London, England, she had had to carry her son and his stroller up and down stairs when traveling on the London metro. A grueling experience shared by many mothers pushing strollers.

The number of *perekhod* decreased as you traveled to the suburbs. As traffic was rarely clear both ways it was common to see people standing on the line halfway across a busy road waiting for the opportunity to get to the other side. We called it the "Russian" maneuver and used it frequently. You just had to stand very still while on the line so as not to distract the drivers and trust that the drivers really did not want to hit you.

******

There were rules when traveling on the metro. Talking to strangers was not done. Speaking loudly raised eyebrows and talking about insignificant things to your friends while on the train was deemed silly. The lack of conversations was noticeable, unlike traveling on the metros in Paris and London. Regular commuters wore subdued colors with black being the favourite. People wearing colorful clothing and baseball hats were foreigners, easy marks for pickpockets and con men. Michael and I bought dark clothes, coats, and hats and learned not to be too conspicuous when riding the metro. We got so good at blending in that occasionally we would be asked for directions by Russians.

The Moscow metro moved millions of people every day and it was so efficient that trains would come every minute during the busiest times. The sheer volume of passengers on the trains during rush hour made the stations crowded. Michael and I learned the "penguin walk," a slow shuffling pace used in the crowds coming off the metro and moving towards the escalator. I would go first and Michael would be directly behind to prevent us getting separated by the pressure of the crowd. Once on the escalator everyone stood on the right to enable the patrons in a rush to run up the left side. If we forgot to stand on the right the staff monitoring the escalators would remind us on the overhead speakers or we risked being pushed out of the way.

During rush hour the metro stations were so crowded that I worried about elderly people getting crushed or knocked over. Luckily, commuters were very aware of people who were not walking as fast or having difficulty with bags or young children. Michael and I witnessed Good Samaritan behaviour on many occasions. Women with children were always given priority and put to the front of lines, as were the elderly. On the trains, younger travelers would quickly offer their seats to those who they thought needed it. When my mother and father came to visit in 2006, they were impressed when they were offered seats. They were over seventy at the time and they welcomed the opportunity to sit even though they were capable of standing.

******

When they visited Moscow Michael and I gave my parents a quick introduction to the metro system. A city map, with key destinations highlighted, allowed them to go sightseeing while we were working. My parents took the metro to the Old Arbat, the Kremlin, as well as Gorky Park. When they needed help the locals were more than happy to send them in the correct direction. Being below ground was a bit disorientating. Often it was difficult to figure out which way to walk when you exited the stations as all the buildings looked the same. On their first trip back to our apartment my parents walked the wrong way for about a kilometre before they thought to ask a local if they were close to our building. Using the map and hand gestures they were quickly pointed in the right direction. After doing the same ourselves Michael and I bought a compass to help us determine our position when we traveled by metro.

I always felt safe when we walked in Moscow. We did not go out at night very often and there were always people on the streets walking to and from the metro and bus stops during the day. The underground *perekhod* shops were open and though there were beggars, they were not threatening. The majority of Russians were honest and kind, but we were careful with our belongings and made sure that we did not stick out in the crowd. We put our wallets and identification inside our coats so they were not easy to steal.

Because of the chance of police spot checks on the streets and at metro stations, Michael and I always carried our passports and paperwork with us. Police security checks at metro entrances increased when the conflict with Chechnya escalated. At these times, Michael was often asked to produce his passport. He was tall and had a mixture of Chinese and German features that were identifiably foreign, but could be confused with people from the far eastern parts of Russia as well as Chechnya.

******

On our trips to Izmaylovo I started buying original paintings, painted boxes, and pottery. I loved the beauty and details of the pieces and wanted to support the artists. Many of my friends and family members were artists. I knew how hard it was to survive on this source of income. A world-renowned artist who specialized in etchings, Alexander Vetrov, was a yearly participant in the Anglo-American Schools winter craft fair. He created etchings of traditional Russian houses and churches. Michael and I purchased an etching each year we were there. When I researched how to make an etching I became more appreciative of the time and effort this man took to make his beautiful pictures.

There were other painters at the school fair, but I preferred to make my way to the Old Arbat to find my favourite artists' stall. The pedestrian only street showcased building facades which dated from the 17th and 18th centuries. Portrait painters set up their chairs at the top end of the street and musicians playing to small crowds in the middle. Independent kiosks selling postcards and paintings were strategically placed down the middle of the walking street. On our first trip one of these stalls caught my eye. Farmyard scenes jumped out at me. I particularly liked their intricate detail. The paintings were small and not too expensive, around $35.00 each. I immediately liked the vendor who was friendly, honest, and sincere about the value of the paintings. She told us that the paintings were by her husband, a professor of art at one of the Moscow Universities. We bought a few paintings on that first day and every time Michael and I walked to the Old Arbat we looked for Anna and stopped to see what she had on display. We always bought something when we found her, and she started to give us "deals", which made the experience even better.

Colleagues recommended a framer they had found close to the House of Artists on the second ring road across the street from Gorky Park. Following their instructions, we found the building easily, but we could not see a sign for a frame shop. None of the front entrances were functional and we walked to the side of the building and noticed a gate that was half closed. After squeezing through the gate and walking to the back we noticed a small sign and some steps that led down to a door. A woman came out as we approached it and we decided to go in to see what was there. We opened the door and entered the framing shop.

Samples of picture frames were hanging on the wall and the mat selections were on a small table. The room was not large, and the choices were limited, but it was good enough for our small pieces of art. We saw two ladies through a window opening in the adjoining room. Using hand gestures and our Russian-English dictionary we placed our first order. We even negotiated the date when we would pick up the pictures by pointing at the calendar. Over the next five years we returned to this framing shop again and again as the prices were extremely reasonable, often less than $5.00 USD per frame. The cost included backing, matting, the frame itself, and the glass. We framed well over fifty paintings during our five years in Moscow.

The House of Artists was within easy walking distance from the framers. It was a contemporary art gallery, which provided space for guest artists as well as Russian artists. When we showed our residence card at the entrance, we paid the local rates. These were half of the tourist rates. One of the perks of being a teacher with a work visa was that we received discounts for all the museums and galleries in the country as well as tickets for ballets and folk-dance companies.

Beside the main gallery there was a large outside park dedicated to sculptors. Walking in this park we found rows of Lenin busts collected from cities all over Russia, in addition to some pretty unusual installations. My favourite was trees carved to look like humans. The displays in the sculptor park were changed regularly and we were always pleasantly surprised.

******

Badminton

One of the best experiences Michael and I had during our time in Moscow was meeting and being coached by a world class badminton player. Marina won the silver medal at the 2000 European Badminton Championships. She was one of the top four women singles players in the world. Training in Sweden, she had dual citizenship, and had represented Sweden in women's singles at the 2004 Olympic Games. A knee injury forced her to retire from the tournament circuit and she returned to Moscow where her family lived. On her return she found employment with the Russian Badminton Federation as a coach and trainer.

Michael and I had met each other playing badminton at a club in Comox, British Columbia. We were both tournament level players. While we completed our Masters' degrees in Victoria we took lessons and played regularly at the Cordova Bay Club. Hard work and practice improved our game to the point that by

2004 we were one of the top, over-35-mixed-doubles teams on Vancouver Island.

Before we left for Moscow Michael contacted a badminton player who lived there. Mikhail turned out to be a wonderful person and a lifelong friend. Mikhail agreed to take us to a competitive club that he knew. The first place he took us to was a university complex in the south end of the city. When we arrived the players were not exactly sure what to do with us. We did not speak Russian and were not part of their club. Mikhail managed to get us onto a court for a few games. We returned to this venue a few times, but the time it took to get there outweighed the few games we were able to play.

I was surprised by the state of disrepair of these university facilities. The building was old, needed painting, and the woman's changing room I was told to use was in a sorry state. There was no running water in the sinks and most of the toilets were broken.

Next, we tried another community center closer to where we lived. Unfortunately, it was a men's group and I was not allowed to play. Michael went regularly. By the end of the first year, he and Mikhail played as partners in a few local tournaments.

In May Mikhail discovered that private courts could be rented at the Palace of Sports located downtown. This was good news. The three of us could use our court time to do drills and play games so that my skills did not decline any further. When we returned to Moscow in August Michael asked his assistant to call the Russian Badminton Federation to inquire about renting a court twice a week and possibly arranging lessons with a coach. When Michael was asked if he would like an English-speaking coach, he agreed enthusiastically. The English-speaking coach was Marina and so started four years of playing and training together, which improved our games considerably.

Michael and I drove to the Palace of Sports to play with Marina and Mikhail twice a week. The Palace of Sports was one of the buildings within the Luzhniki sports complex that had been used for the 1980 Olympics. On the left side of the second floor there was a room big enough to house one indoor tennis court or four badminton courts. Both sets of lines were painted on the floor and courts were rented out yearly in two-hour slots. The main arena was small and used for events like ballroom dance competitions and dog shows. Usually there was nothing going on in the arena. The four of us and a few other avid badminton players were the only ones in the building.

It was always a bit of an adventure getting into this complex. We paid for a special car pass which allowed us to enter through a little-known security gate on the river side of the complex and park at the Palace of Sports building. The side gate was convenient. We could avoid traffic going to concerts and sports events held at the larger Stadium. The amount of security at our gate depended on the political situation in Georgia and Chechnya as well as what events were being held at the Stadium. Sometimes we were waved through without any issues, other times there were armed guards, trunk checks, and mirrors used to look under the car for explosives. There was never a dull moment during our adventures outside the expat bubble in Moscow.

Over four years Michael and I got stronger and fitter with improvements to our strokes and footwork that subsequently wowed our friends back in BC. Our physical activity was not cheap, the court was $50.00 an hour, and we booked it for two hours on Tuesdays and Thursdays. Marina's fee was also $50.00 an hour, plus the cost of the badminton birds we used. Michael calculated that we spent at least $15,000 a year for this physical exercise and entertainment. Luckily our salaries supported our habit. Mikhail and Marina became good friends and we spent time with them outside the badminton court. We went out for dinner regularly and Michael and I went to Marina's parent's dachas for a weekend in the fall. Marina and Mikhail traveled to British Columbia during the summer of 2009 and we took them to Tofino to see whales, sea otters, and eagles. A driving tour through the mountains of southern B.C. completed their holiday.

*****

Exploring Russia

During one of the school holidays Michael and I drove from Moscow to St. Petersburg, a distance of five hundred kilometres. Based on our experiences driving across Canada we calculated the trip would take between five and six hours. Since the highway was the major land link between the two cities, we were confident that it would be well maintained. We were wrong.

Michael and I knew that very few people on our route would be able to speak English, so we asked Mikhail to accompany us on the trip. He agreed. He had never been to St. Petersburg and wanted to see the historical sights. We booked a bed and breakfast and our overall plan for the week was to spend one day in the Hermitage and go to the Church on Spilled Blood and the Peter and Paul fortress. We also wanted to visit the Queen Anne and Peterhof Palaces, both day trips from St. Petersburg.

Our small party set out in the morning with the plan to stop halfway for lunch and have dinner in St. Petersburg. The road was a four-lane highway for about an hour at which point it decreased to a two-lane road with the occasional third uncontrolled passing lane. Transport trucks were in various states of repair, and some had very distinct tilts, likely due to being loaded improperly. To our surprise, the highway did not bypass towns. We drove through each one at 50 km/hr, which added to our travel time substantially. At noon we started looking for a place for lunch. After going through three or four towns we finally saw a restaurant sign hanging from the door of a dilapidated building at the edge of a truck stop parking lot. At this point we had no option other than go into the restaurant—we needed to use the washrooms, and get something to eat.

The waitress brought us menus written in Cyrillic. Mikhail translated each item in exhausting detail to help us make our selections. Little did he know that by the time he read out the tenth item I had forgotten the first three. I was too polite to say anything. After all, his purpose was to help us make an informed choice. While Mikhail translated, I looked around the restaurant and decided that the kitchen's health and safety record might not be up to the standard my innards were accustomed to.

Intestinal health was a frequent topic during school lunches. Bouts of diarrhea from drinking contaminated water or eating poorly cooked food were common and we were very careful when traveling and eating out. I knew that soup and bread would be the best option in this situation and directed Mikhail's translation task to the soup choices. I decided on Borscht, but further down the list was one called *piti* soup which tweaked Michael's interest. Mikhail explained that it was a mutton soup with vegetables and beans. The waitress told him that it was a local favourite and very popular. With this endorsement they ordered the soup.

My borsch came in a bowl, but the *piti* soup was served in ceramic clay containers which added to the authenticity of the peasant meal. Michael and Mikhail spooned the soup into the bowls that were provided. The first spoonful was a clear broth with onions and carrots. The next provided some chickpeas and vegetables. Wondering where the mutton was Michael took one more dip into the soup pot and a large piece of white gelatinous material appeared on his spoon. This evoked looks of wonder and disgust—it looked nothing like meat, vegetable or bean. The jiggling mass was animal fat and one of many found at the bottom of each container. It turned out that *piti* soup's key ingredient was mutton fat, which might have been a delicacy for some, but not us.

******

As we continued our trip north the road got worse. Construction detours and slowdowns became a common occurrence. We started to worry about getting to St. Petersburg by nightfall. At one point we stopped for gas, but Michael had no idea how to activate the pumps. Mikhail read the signs and gave Michael a quick explanation. Michael then walked up to the tiny booth to prepay. You always had to prepay for gas. He called out the pump number and how much gas he wanted in Russian. The attendant responded with a question that Michael couldn't understand. A worrying event as in the past Michael had been verbally abused by gas attendants when he said the wrong thing or did not know what to do. In these cases a friendly person in the queue would volunteer to help Michael so that they could get their gas in a timely fashion. Michael was pleasantly surprised when the attendant came out of the gas cabin miming that the pump we wanted was not working. He was very forgiving of the fact that Michael could not speak much Russian.

While Michael and Mikhail were filling up the car, I witnessed what appeared to be a septic truck dumping its load straight into the stream that ran behind the gas station. Being a biology teacher and nurse the action shocked me. I found, in general, Russians were not as ecologically minded as Europeans, possibly because Russia was such a big country with lots of places to dump garbage without directly affecting people.

******

St. Petersburg had been designed and built by Peter the Great and was the capital of Russia until 1918. He incorporated the same strategy as Amsterdam to channel the waters of the swampy estuary. Canals and bridges were everywhere. As we walked the streets, we saw an intriguing mixture of modern architecture built alongside the old. The three major palaces, the Hermitage, Peterhof (a short boat ride away), and the Palace of Tsarskoye Selo were built by the ruling Tsars; we visited them all.

Before smart phones and easy Wi-Fi access, we used tourist books, which included maps to find the places we wanted to see. The one we consulted contained pictures and descriptions of the historical highlights of the city. We used it to find a bridge with white lions holding a guardrail supports and a beautiful church with domes coated with gold leaf.

After a good night's sleep, we walked to the Hermitage. The Hermitage was a truly gargantuan building. The winter palace of the Romanov Tsar's, there were no signs indicating an entrance gate for pedestrian visitors. Mikhail asked at the tour bus entrance and we were directed to an entrance around the back for locals and people with residence cards. This door would have been the service entrance for the palace. Once inside the museum we were free to wander around at will and we saw things that most tour groups did not. Tour groups from Moscow or cruise ships had strict timelines and they only saw the famous paintings and statues before getting back on their buses. As we were not bound by time, we wandered around for most of the day enjoying the very eclectic and extensive collections that the museum displayed.

Full of paintings and other treasures from Russia's illustrious past, the collections we saw ranged from old pieces of jewelry to sculptures from Egypt and the ancient world. The walls of the rooms were decorated with gold plated molding and paintings. Peter the Great and his successor Catherine the Great commissioned European artists to do paintings to be displayed in St. Petersburg. The influence of Versailles could be seen everywhere and there were indeed exact copies of well-known statues in prominent places. The permanent painting collections were priceless and in an odd twist one of the temporary exhibitions contained the works of an artist from Montreal, Canada.

Next to the Hermitage was St. Isaac's Cathedral, built in 1858. The walls and ceilings were beautifully decorated, and the floors were tiled with marble slabs of varying colours and patterns. We climbed two hundred and sixty-two steps to the top of the dome and looked at the panoramic views of the city. In the distance the docks reminded us that St. Petersburg was a cosmopolitan city with ties to Europe and the rest of the world. The attitude on the streets towards foreigners was more relaxed than in Moscow. I attributed this to the fact that the locals interacted with foreigners frequently, so we were not so much of a surprise.

The next day we walked to the Peter and Paul fortress. The majority of Romanov Tsars were buried in tombs at the large Cathedral within the fortress. The star shaped fortress was surrounded by water. As we crossed the bridge there was an imposing sign at the entrance instructing us what we could and could not do while visiting the fortress. There were three rows of the familiar red circle with a cross forbidding the specific behaviours drawn within them.

Some of the activities were obvious, like not lighting fires, but others had us scratching our heads. It appeared that you were not allowed to play brass instruments or step off the top of the buildings. One figure of a stylized man in a bathing suit had the universal cross through it. We decided that swimming was forbidden even though common sense showed there was nowhere to enter the water other than jumping off the walls. Another picture showed a man pushing over a tree and another looked like a man skiing. We would never know what strange events had prompted these specific warnings.

We took the tour boat from the center of town to the palace of Peterhof as it was quicker than driving up the coastal road. The boat trip was a bit of an adventure—the boat looked like something from the 1960s. Sleek and shiny with a jet engine strapped onto the back. Noisy and smelly the boat rose up on its hydroplane skis and transported us to the destination in thirty-five minutes.

The impressive Peterhof gardens were similar to the ones built at Versailles, France. We entered the estate at the bottom of the Grand Cascade fountain. It had multiple levels and was lined with golden statues spurting water in all directions. The fountain did not require pumps as the whole thing worked on gravity and was an engineering marvel. The site map showed many smaller fountains, as well as kilometers of garden paths to explore within the estate.

After looking at the Grand Cascade fountains we headed to the main palace. At the ticket booth we found the rules were different for the palace. At the Hermitage, Michael and I were allowed to enter as locals with our residence cards, but the same rule did not apply at Peterhof. Mikhail was a Russian citizen and he was not allowed to enter at the foreigner door. We were foreigners and even though we had resident cards we could not go in the Russian citizen door. When we asked if we could go in separately to meet on the inside we were told that the palace tour routes were completely separate for locals and foreigners. Michael and I did not think it a good idea to separate. No matter how hard we tried, there was no arguing that our "mixed" group would be fine using the local entrance. Our papers did not match the rules the ticket seller was using. Giving up we enjoyed the beautiful gardens before catching the boat back to the city.

On our final day in St. Petersburg, we ventured out to see the Church of the Savior on Spilled Blood, one of the most beautiful churches in Russia and possibly in the world. The church was built over the exact spot where Tsar Alexander II was assassinated in 1880 and the mosaics, which covered the walls and ceilings, surpassed the ones in St. Mark's Cathedral in Venice. The builders purposely left the cobblestones where the assassination occurred in place and there was a small tent-like structure surrounding the spot. It was striking to see this simple memorial in the middle of the magnificently decorated church.

Outside the onion domes were magical, a combination of gold and multicolored swirls. They were even more ornate than St. Basil's in Red Square and the church was bigger. In addition, the Church of the Savior on Spilled Blood was located on a smaller canal which allowed people to take pictures from all angles.

******

We drove to see Catherine the Great's palace on the way back to Moscow. The palace was a few kilometers south of St. Petersburg and we got there early. At the entrance-gate to the estate were the usual kiosks that sold birch bark trinkets and *matryoshka* or nesting dolls. There were no issues at the local ticket booth with our credentials and we were allowed to go in together.

The palace was destroyed in WWII and what we were walking through was a complete restoration based on architectural drawings and pictures. An impressive undertaking, restoration included finding enough amber to line a small room, sourcing Flemish fireplaces, and commissioning all the reproductions of ceiling and wall art as well as the furniture. The main palace was a series of joined ballrooms stretching for about half a kilometre with smaller bedroom suites at one end. The locals' route was down one side of the grand rooms, and the tourists had a route on the other side. There was no mixing of the two groups. Each room had a placard describing its function and Mikhail translated them for us as we moved along.

The ornate façade of the palace was decorated with wrought iron balcony rails and statues that were in the process of being gold plated. Like the palaces of France, the estate included several gardens, out buildings, and a large lake. Many families had brought picnics with them, and they were spread out on the grass between the flower beds enjoying the nice weather.

******

As we were driving back to Moscow, we noticed people sitting behind portable tables at the side of the road. They were selling tea using water heated in samovars as well as wild mushrooms and other freshly harvested vegetables. Occasionally we saw a single light bulb hanging from a tree by a path to a house. These were a mystery. No one was in sight and sometimes the bulb was on and sometimes it was not. Mikhail didn't know what they were selling, but he thought it looked suspicious. Later we were told by other Russian friends that these houses sold fake receipts to truck drivers. In St. Petersburg they would pick up a shipment and, on their way home, stop and get fake receipts for more than they had paid for the shipment. When they delivered the shipment, they pocketed the extra cash.

******

On our return trip, we had difficulty finding somewhere to eat. The *piti* soup truck stop had been demolished due to road construction. Further down the highway, Mikhail finally saw a sign that advertised a resort complex with a restaurant. We followed the signs to a Russian style sanatorium spa beside a lake.

Mikhail talked to the guard at the gate and we were allowed to go to the cafeteria. We did not see any other people in the restaurant and the waiter was surprised to see us enter. Both were bad signs. The menu was extensive, but given our past experience with restaurants we asked what was available from the menu. All the kitchen was able to make was ham sandwiches with sliced cucumbers and tomatoes. We enjoyed our sandwiches and were soon back on the highway to Moscow.

******

Sergiev Posad and the Golden Ring

The small town of Sergiev Posad was a popular tourist destination. An hour's drive northeast of the outer ring road it was a UNESCO world heritage site known for its blue domed churches and monasteries. Sergiev Posad was part of the "Golden

Ring," a group of eight cities that played a role in the beginnings of the Russian Orthodox Church. Most of the cities were outdoor museums, but the cathedrals at Sergiev Posad were fully operational places of worship. Viewed from outside the starred blue domes of the orthodox Russian cathedrals and churches were incredibly picturesque. Inside, the churches had colorful wall paintings and mosaics.

The first time we went to Sergiev Posad, Michael and I were with a group of new teachers on a tour organized by the school. We stopped at some of the small kiosks and bought our first traditional birch bark boxes. I looked longingly at the colorfully painted laminated boxes, but they were more expensive than the birch bark ones. This was the start of my collection of small birch bark boxes.

Sergiev Posad was just being developed for tour groups in 2004 and there were few restaurants that could serve many people at the same time. The tour company provided bag lunches for us, and we ate them in one of the parks overlooking the monastery complexes.

After our first trip, Michael and I drove to Sergiev Posad two more times with friends. We loved seeing the religious artifacts and medieval art found in the various monasteries. The last time we drove to Sergeiv Posad, we went to pick up a hand-carved wooden staff. We had ordered it to be made at the school craft fair in December and arranged to collect the completed staff in the spring.

We were accompanied by friends who had also ordered staffs from the artist. After picking up our wooden staffs we went in search of place to eat lunch. We saw a small sign for a *pelmeni* (dumpling) restaurant. The restaurant was tiny, but looked clean. The menu was a single sheet of paper with five choices of *pelmeni* fillings. When we asked if they served anything else they said no. The other place in town only sold fried chicken. We decided to order a variety of *pelmeni,* which were tasty. The total charge was a few dollars each, very different from the usual fifty dollar bills we paid in Moscow.

******

In our fifth and last year in Russia we drove to "Goose Crystalnee" or if correctly written, Gus Khrustalny with Karen and Mark. Founded in 1756 it was the largest city producing crystal glassware in Russia. Karen and Mark had driven to Gus Khrustalny before and noticed that the prices were much lower than if we bought the same crystal at Izmaylovo. The crystal patterns were traditional, classy, and half the price of Irish Waterford crystal.

We left for Gus Khrustalny in the afternoon relying on the junior school's personal assistants verbal and hand-written instructions. The city was a three-hour drive away and only a small dot on our map of Russia. Being optimists, we were confident that the city would be well signposted. As we drove along the highway the local farm stands selling tea and spring vegetables became more numerous. The weather was good, the drive scenic with a backdrop of birch trees and blue skies. The first exit off the highway showed Gus Khrustalny written clearly on the signage. The next intersection was confusing and we had to rely on our hand-drawn map. We turned right and started doubting our decision when the next intersection on the map did not appear as quickly as expected. Mark remained confident that we were on the right track. As the minutes went by the rest of us had misgivings. There was no indication that a large town would appear soon; if anything we were getting further away from civilization.

Karen was worried that we were going to get really lost if we did not stop to ask for directions. We insisted that Mark stop the car when we saw two women walking along the side of the road. Karen rolled down her window and asked in her best Russian if they knew the way to Gus Khrustalny. At first they did not understand a word Karen was saying. To help, Mark and Michael both tried pronouncing Gus Khrustalny in a way they thought would be close to the actual pronunciation. After many attempts, the women finally understood and started to talk amongst themselves.

We listened politely to their instructions, understanding about ten percent of the words and about fifty percent of the sign language. With smiles and waves, we turned around and headed back the way we had come. As the discussion had not really helped us, we decided to go back to the intersection where we had turned right and take one of the other two remaining options. Luckily our next choice was the correct one and we saw the hotel within ten minutes.

When she booked the hotel, the personal assistant warned us that the hotel was Soviet era and not to expect a five-star establishment. The hotel was located on the only road into town and the four-story brick building had a simple sign that said "hotel" in Russian hanging on the outside, *gostinitsa* or гостиница in Cyrillic. The building could have been a factory or an apartment block — they all followed the same basic plans. The entrance was a little unusual. When we opened the door we found ourselves in a large room with chairs lining the walls and nothing else. It was very quiet and there was no one in sight. We crossed the room and walked through a door on the other side. In this second room we found the registration desk and we checked in without any issues. The rooms were basic and functional, and we settled in to eat our picnic dinner. We had packed food as we knew that restaurants were hard to find in small towns.

When we went down for breakfast the server was surprised to see us. It seemed that most guests slept in and missed breakfast. As it was the choices were minimal. The only things on the table were cereal and milk, toast and jam, as well as, plates of sliced cucumbers, and salami.

After eating we drove to the market. It was very similar to the Gorbushka open air market, but not as large. There were about six rows of small stores with individuals selling crystal glasses and other types of glassware and ceramics. These included garden gnomes and large-scale vases with the tackiest of patterns. Karen and Mark purchased some glasses and resisted the gnomes even though we thought they would be perfect for their house in Canada. Michael and I bought glasses of different sizes and styles to be stored for our return to Canada.

As we walked through the market Michael noticed a large banner hanging from the side of a building. On the banner a model was wearing a bikini as well as a fur vest and boots. It was hard to guess what the advertisement was for, but Michael was struck by the contrast. The difference between the opulence depicted on the banner and the reality of what we were walking through was extreme. The market was old with collapsing and rundown buildings filled with older people trying to sell factory surpluses. This was likely their bonus and only means of making any extra money. No one in this city, other than the owners of the factories, could afford what was advertised on that poster.

We carefully loaded our new glassware into the back of the car and drove half an hour north towards Vladimir and Suzdal, two historic cities belonging to the "Golden Ring." Vladimir had many old orthodox churches as well as historical buildings. It was considered the spiritual center of Russia and its prominent church was built with distinctive red brick. Vladimir catered to day tours from Moscow, so there were a few restaurants open for lunch. The one we picked was decorated like a garden with plastic sunflower plants and grapevines woven into the rafters. We all enjoyed soup and sandwiches before driving on to Suzdal.

Suzdal had many different styles of churches and monasteries. Their gold and blue starred domes reached towards the sky. I saw three young men dressed like knights on their way to either the re-enactment of a battle or to pose with tourists. The churches and buildings had been there for centuries. A UNESCO world heritage site, most of the old houses were restored and lived in by locals. We spent time at an art exhibit located in one of the church buildings. There were exquisite wooden carvings inspired by religious as well as mythical figures. The church interior was striking with its painted walls and mosaics in the floors reminiscent of Roman ruins.

The town's recreation of an earlier time was complemented by horse drawn carriages and a musician playing an accordion on the walking path. Like a scene out of a painting, a cat sat beside a young fisherman on a small footbridge waiting for a fish to be caught. It was a peaceful and idyllic lifestyle, which we left behind as we drove back to the big city of Moscow.

******

Banya Experience

Russians loved saunas. Public bath houses could be found in most districts. Michael and I did not venture into the bath houses. When we heard about a traditional Russian banya experience that included a horse-drawn sleigh ride, we decided to give it a try. The 'spa' was located outside of Moscow and the banya package included transportation there and back, as well as lunch, dinner, and the sauna. The highlight for Michael would be the jump into a freezing cold creek after heating up in the sauna.

We gathered a small group of friends and booked the day trip. The weather was sunny and cold. On the way the van stopped at a hill where we were given the opportunity to toboggan. The snow was fresh and fluffy. Everyone had a great time laughing as we climbed, slipping and sliding, back up the hill. After a few runs we continued to the house to find brightly decorated horse-drawn sleighs. Settling under blankets we were pulled along a forest trail, the sleigh bells ringing and the horses snorting. After a short while we stopped in a clearing where a large fire was burning. The fire pit was surrounded by chairs and we were told to sit and cover ourselves with blankets.

Lunch was served at this clearing and I learned my first Russian word, "chute-chute" (чуть-чуть) meaning "just a little bit." As we cooked our hotdogs over the fire and ate some pickles, our host offered us vodka in plastic cups. He was generous with the quantities of vodka being poured into our large cups. I continually had to say, "just a little bit," as I did not want to drink too much at lunch time.

Returning to the house we went to the sauna area and put on our bathing suits. Before we entered the sauna our host unexpectedly covered us in a honey rub. Supposedly the honey was medicinal as it opened skin pores. After ten to fifteen minutes of steam we were instructed to jump into a cold pool next to the sauna or go outside and jump in the ice-hole cut into the creek.

I was not that keen on running across snow, so I opted for the cold pool. Michael, of course, chose the river route. By this time we were all well plied with vodka. The cold water was invigorating, but we quickly ran back to the steam room to warm up.

We lay down on the benches in the sauna and the attendant lightly hit us with bows of birch leaves mixed with a fragrant herb that smelt like camphor. The "beating" was to increase circulation and improve our health. After another ten to fifteen minutes of steam, we returned to the cold pool or river for relief. We repeated this routine two more times before it was time for dinner. The man who beat us with birch boughs wore the most amazing felt hat that was soaking wet. He told us that it was the only way to stay cool in the sauna while hitting us with the tree boughs.

After showers we dressed and sat down for a traditional Russian meal. It included borscht, *pelmeni*, sliced meats, salad, and potatoes. The alcohol continued to flow, and the drunkest member of our group had the honour of wearing a bear skin shawl during the Russian circle dancing. All this revelry was topped with some Karaoke (a Russian passion) before we all piled back into the van for our return journey to Moscow. The banya became popular with many of our expatriate colleagues. When the hosts had a house fire, in which one of the brothers died, donations were quickly raised so that they could restart the business.

******

Teaching at the Anglo-American School of Moscow

Michael and I became good friends with the musical brothers who had filled his position for a year. Neither one had the western credentials required by the school to be hired permanently as teachers. When Michael arrived, one was hired as Michael's assistant and the other gave lessons after school. Through conversations with them we started to understand some of the more unique Russian ways of thinking. An example of this occurred when we could not understand what was being asked of us at a restaurant and the server became aggressive. A quick call to our new friends confirmed for the waiter that we wanted rice with our meal rather than potatoes. The waiter thought we were idiots for not understanding his question. Rice, in his mind, was unacceptable.

The Soviet teaching style was autocratic and skills based. Students did what the teacher told them without question. The expectation of blind obedience was a good example of cultural differences between education systems. Raising voices and telling students that they were no good was considered a motivator; a method of showing what could be done better. Unbeknownst to Russian teachers, children from other cultures found the technique "mean" and de-motivating.

The use of this methodology caused problems on the grade six week-without-walls trip. Our Russian guide, who was a wonderful man, would raise his voice and say things to embarrass the students who were reluctant to try new things. The instructor's intentions were well-intentioned, but the outcome was not what he expected. Our foreign students were not motivated, and embarrassed to be singled out. At one point when some students were in tears, I stepped forward to suggest alternative techniques for these "coddled westerners." The tour guide was happy to try them as he wanted the students to enjoy the trip. With a few subtle changes the tone of the trip improved. The students were willing to engage in new things when the task became a group effort rather than a competition.

The teaching facilities at the Anglo-American School of Moscow were world class and my middle school classroom had brand new science tables and stations with working sinks. Gas connections for Bunsen burners existed, but to my surprise they were not attached to a gas supply. I was told that the city of Moscow did not allow the storage of natural gas on school property so I could not use the Bunsen burners. I immediately ordered hot plates and used alcohol burners or candles if I needed a flame. Moscow taught me to be flexible and creative in planning practical experiences—many things commonly used in Canadian classrooms were not often available.

Though the classrooms and main buildings were completed, the school was a construction zone for three years while the theatre was finished and the pool built. Most of the unskilled laborers were poorly dressed and undoubtedly poorly paid. The materials used to build the walls were of questionable quality and they were moved by wheelbarrows and bucket lines. Rickety scaffolding with no safety lines contrasted unfavourably with western construction sites regulated by workers compensation boards.

As the work on the theatre and pool continued the only inconvenience was the unplanned fire alarms. The alarms were triggered inadvertently by construction related smoke or heat and occurred once or twice each semester. A few of the fire alarms happened in the middle of winter. Below zero temperatures and half a metre of snow forced the administration to think about plans for a real disaster where students would have to be moved somewhere warm. Ironically the closest building to the school was a crematorium.

When the school had been built each room had brackets for TVs, which took three years to appear. The non-existent TVs were a bit of a joke and some teachers put boxes with "coming soon" signs on them in the blank space. When the TVs were installed, teachers were at a loss as to how to use them for educational purposes. The TV's were not connected to a closed circuit system and video-on-demand was in its infancy.

Determined to make use of the television in the corner of my room I asked for a CD/DVD player. The machine was supplied, but the technicians attached the player to the TV with cables so short that the machine had to be placed on a shelf well above my reach. Obviously, the cable wires were in short supply, so I stood on a chair to put the DVDs into the player.

When the science team asked for more computers the IT director said it was not possible because the school had run out of electricity. The school was a brand-new building. Unfortunately, the builders had not foreseen the exponential growth of technology or the subsequent need for more electricity when they negotiated the original power supply with the district's electrical company. A second power cable needed to be installed from the city's grid before more computers could be plugged in.

In my travels I found electrical hazards were given different priorities. Dangling electrical cords were not seen as a problem in Moscow, Bangladesh or the United Arab Emirates. In Moscow, six computers were placed at the back of my room. To get electricity the service men accessed a power line in the ceiling and dangled electrical cords from the ceiling directly to the computers. This situation presented a hazard as students walking by could catch the cord, trip and pull the computers off the tables. After a year of complaining the computers were finally wired in safely.

When I walked into my Moscow classroom at the beginning of my second year, I found a phone placed in the middle of a student desk at the front of the room. Phones had been put in all classrooms as a security measure for potential lockdown situations. When I asked why the phone was not on my desk the answer was that the phone cord did not reach that far. The workmen did not have the authority to cut a longer cord and had continued on to the next room.

To solve the problem of not having a long enough cord I rearranged the classroom furniture to put my desk where the phone reached. It was better to work around the problem than get angry. A classroom phone was an example of an administration solving a problem that did not exist—I never used mine. Phone extension codes were buried within administration documents that no one used. If I wanted to talk to my teaching colleagues, I walked to their rooms or met them during the lunch breaks.

There were no phones in my classrooms in Bangladesh, Thailand, or the UAE. My classroom phone in South Korea was located on the demonstration desk at the front of the classroom. It also did not have enough cable to put it anywhere else. The phone rang one day and I suddenly realized that I did not know which button to push to connect with the caller. By the time I had pushed all the buttons the caller had hung up. In over twenty years of teaching, only two incidents required phoning out to get help; both were calls for ambulances and I used a mobile phone.

******

For me, the most challenging aspect of teaching in Moscow was the procurement of school supplies. I was always planning lessons with limited resources. Items coming into Russia would either disappear at the border or a heavy fee needed to be paid. Our choir teacher ordered sheet music through the mail and the "tax" was more than the papers were worth. To circumvent the border issues the school used the American Embassy's diplomatic service for all imports.

Diplomatic shipments had immunity from tax and tariffs and could not be stopped at the border. The school ordered all materials, including educational books, from the United States once a year. In October, supplies were ordered by department and sent to procurement to be approved. Once ordered the materials did not arrive until the next school year started. It was not easy to predict what you might need eight months in advance.

The general order for science included glassware, equipment, and chemicals. Specific items for experiments were requested by individual teachers. Teachers arriving in August would receive boxes of materials that the previous teachers had ordered before they had decided to leave. Usually the resources made sense, but I found things in the back storerooms that could not be used in the middle school curriculum. I donated owl pellets and other interesting "items" to the junior school in order to clear the storage space.

One of the most surprising rooms at the school was the art and crafts office supply room located in the basement. This room always had stationery and art supplies, but as the year went by the number of items like colored paper and glue sticks decreased. Some teachers were hoarders and would take more than their share. Occasionally, everyone was instructed to return their unused supplies to the room for a thorough stock taking.

The person who ran the supply room ordered from various catalogs and it was a bit like Christmas. You were never sure what you would find, and this uncertainty stimulated my creativity. I would go down for pens and papers and come back with materials that I could use for experiments and other activities in my science classes.

******

Classroom management was not a problem—parents and administration supported teachers. Everyone worked together to help the students achieve their potential. Teaching the children of billionaires could present a challenge, and often entailed special considerations. Children of wealthy families were experienced travelers. Frequently they flew on private jets to Paris or London for a weekend of shopping or to the Alps for skiing, but they were not good at looking after themselves. They had nannies and drivers to do this.

Many of the students came to school in motorcades of black Audi's. One had a convoy of four Hummers and an armed security detail that waited outside the school all day. Her team of bodyguards discretely accompanied us on field trips within the city as well as on the extended field trips.

One student had his own apartment with the appropriate compliment of servants who looked after him while his parents were away on business trips. After a few months of teaching, I realized that his parents rarely saw him. Wealthy children could display the same signs of emotional neglect as those with alcoholic or abusive parents. In some cases, drivers or guardians brought gifts and received updates on student's progress during the parent-teacher conferences.

The grade sixes went on an extended field trip at the end of the school year. Without their parents, the students had to be more responsible for their own belongings. After recovering from the fact that the hotels were not 5-star, students were shown how to pack their own small suitcase. They were instructed that they would be responsible for carrying their bags on and off the buses and trains. The number of bags left on the sidewalk beside the buses on the first day made us laugh. Before we moved in or out of hotel reception areas the teachers would always ask the group who had "forgotten" their belongings. The students all improved by the end of the trip.

The grade six extended field trip began with an overnight train to Novgorod, a city just south of St. Petersburg. The train was old and slow. It stopped many times along the way. Each car had an attendant who checked our tickets and was in charge of the hot water machine. The attendants were not to be dealt with lightly. Some were downright rude, and they were not pleased when twenty-four excited twelve-year-olds piled into the six berths of their train car. We made it a habit of giving them a good tip at the end as they were going to have to work harder to clean the rooms. Even though it was an expectation that the students clean up, there were always the disaster rooms where chips and other fast foods were crushed into the floor.

Once we arrived in Novgorod the group split into two and hired guides took us on independent circle tours of Novgorod, Pskov, Pushkin's estates and Pechory. Russian speaking teachers were assigned to each group to communicate with hotel front desks and to troubleshoot any problems that came up. On the first trip, we learned that the hotels would not return our passports before all the towels in the rooms had been tallied. On a few occasions, our departure was delayed while the counting was done and redone. Needless to say, the "towel rule" was part of the orientation for the next year.

The five-day trip had a cultural orientation. The agenda included going to restored forts, numerous old churches, as well as monuments to historical battles. For me, the highlight of the trip was the fifteenth-century monastery in Pechory, located just a few kilometres from the Estonian border. The church complex featured amazing blue and gold cupolas and murals. Underneath the main buildings, tunnels dug in the sandstone ran in many directions. Thousands of monks were buried in this large subterranean catacomb and honoured with services conducted by the monks who lived there.

To enter the gates of the Pechory monastery female students and teachers were given wrap around skirts and headscarves to wear. Men and boys had to wear long pants or they were given the skirts to cover their legs. When entering the tunnels beeswax candles were given to the students and adults to light their way. Following the guide, we walked in a single file passed the closed doors of burial chambers and felt the spiritual importance of the place. The guide stopped at various places to tell the students the history of the older graves.

The candles were designed to last for the short time we were in the caves. Waving them around made them burn faster. The catacombs were pitch black and the screams of anguish as the candles ran out was disconcerting, but also funny as the students huddled around the ones who had listened to the instructions and not waved their candles.

An important part of the trip was the time spent at the tourist stalls set up at the entrances of the churches, forts, and other historical buildings. The children always wanted to purchase souvenirs for their parents and siblings—regional crafts were favoured although a pointed wooden club called a morning star was very popular with the boys. The decorative clubs came in all sizes. Fearing potential injuries, I decided the purchase of the clubs was okay as long as they stayed inside suitcases. The students followed this rule and no accidents occurred.

Field trips with large groups of children always resulted in age appropriate misbehaviour. At one souvenir stall in Novgorod the boys found a small utility knife which doubled as a blow torch. We only discovered they had bought the knife after they set toilet paper alight and threw it out the window of the hotel. Complaints from people living opposite the hotel alerted us to the issue. Luckily no one was hurt and nothing was burnt other than the toilet paper. The blow torch knives were confiscated immediately. Michael and I used them to start barbecues for years.

Using Russian domestic transport was always a bit risky. The trains were old and rickety, but internal flights were worse. Michael accompanied the grade sevens to Sochi. The flight from Moscow to Sochi was on an old converted freight bus. The seats were numbered backwards because in Russia passengers boarded from the back of the plane. Inside the fuselage, the "living quarters" were not fixed at enough contact points so the entire internal fuselage would torque when the plane changed direction. To add to the worry, the walls had missing panels and wires hung out. Many of the seat belts did not work and often the domestic passengers were busy getting drunk. The record amount of alcohol consumed according to Michael was an entire bottle of scotch shared between three men, who disembarked as if they had simply drunk some coffee.

******

Pigeon Holed- Time to move on

Michael and I enjoyed living in Moscow. There was always something to see or do on weekends and our badminton lessons kept us busy during the week. Common experiences pulled us together with our colleagues and we maintained lifelong friendships with many of the people we worked with. The decision to leave was initiated by the narrowmindedness and inexperience of the middle and high school principals. For reasons only known to them they would not consider Michael and I as candidates for other positions within the schools. I had been hired as a middle school science teacher originally teaching grade six and eight, but had been teaching nursing students at the university level before that. I loved the middle school age group, but had started to miss the cognitive abilities of sixteen and seventeen-year-olds.

A grade eleven biology position came vacant during our fourth year. Well qualified to teach this position with my biology and nursing background I hand delivered my resume to the high school principal and verbally expressed my interest in the position. I heard nothing for weeks. I found this slightly insulting. When I decided to ask what was going on, my resume was returned to me unopened. The principal told me that the director had already hired someone to fill the vacancy.

A similar situation occurred with Michael. A vacancy for a middle school computer teacher was posted and he thought that it would be a perfect opportunity to switch out of music, which was affecting his hearing. Michael was qualified for the position as he had been programming and using computer software for years. Michael spoke to both the middle and high school principals, but they refused to consider his request.

We had been pigeon-holed for unknown reasons. Other teachers had moved to different positions in the school the year before. Our inability to move within the school was unexpected and disappointing. In the fall of 2009 we decided to look for work elsewhere. Michael and I signed on with two teacher recruitment agencies, Search Associates and International School Services, to improve our chances. In hindsight the decision to use two agencies was not an advantage.

******

In the mid 2000's the recruitment of international teachers took place at recruitment fairs. The larger fairs were held in Bangkok, London, Kingston, and Boston. We were told by friends that there would be more vacancies available at Bangkok than at London a few weeks later. We later discovered that most of the larger schools sent hiring teams to all the fairs. They interviewed teachers in Bangkok, but did not send out offers until they had interviewed candidates in London and sometimes in North America. In hindsight, there was no advantage to going to Bangkok rather than London.

The school's winter holiday ended when the Bangkok fair began. We planned a holiday in Thailand so we would be rested before the fairs began. The International Schools Service fair was first followed by the Search Associates. The hiring fairs were held in upscale hotels along the river. My parents joined us for the holiday part of the trip and we enjoyed seeing the historical sites as well as the elephant sanctuaries found along the route from Bangkok to Chiangrai.

Chapter 2:
Bangladesh 2009-2011

Michael and I were not thinking of working in Dhaka when we went to the job fair in Bangkok. We were hoping for jobs in Southeast Asia or Europe as there were many vacancies advertised on the recruitment websites. Michael booked rooms at the fair hotels naively thinking that this would be an advantage. In hindsight, we did not meet or discuss anything with the hiring teams outside the recruitment fair hours so where we stayed was immaterial. The benefits were the lack of travel time in the morning and the perks of staying in a five-star hotel. It was convenient to retreat to our room when we had nothing else to do, and the breakfast buffets were impressive.

On our first day in Bangkok, we met with our assigned representative who gave us a quick overview of the process. The hiring season was a huge puzzle of job vacancies and the teachers wishing to fill them. Human resource teams compiled lists of teachers that fit their vacancies and, in some cases, contacted their first choices before the fairs to set interview times.

In the days before Skype and Zoom, face to face interviews occurred in administrator's hotel rooms. Teachers were assigned files which were placed alphabetically in boxes in one of the smaller conference rooms at the hotel. The room was open to anyone walking by. As far as I could tell no one worried about potential tampering. Invitations for interviews were placed in the files by the hiring teams and it was up to the individual to check for invitations. On receipt of an invitation the teacher walked to the schools hiring table and arranged an interview time for the next day. If you did not want to accept an interview you sent the administrators a "thanks, but no thank you" email.

In the main conference room directors, principals and human resource staff sat at tables organized alphabetically. Vacancies were handwritten on poster paper behind the tables. Teachers who had not received an invitation to interview, but were requesting an interview anyway, lined up in front of the tables. I found this rather strange. If I had not received a card in my folder, I assumed I had not been shortlisted and therefore was of no interest to the employer. Many teachers did this for interview practice and the slim chance they might impress the interviewer and be considered for a position later.

Inside the room colourful banners advertised the schools and promotional flyers were available on the tables. Schools were given time slots in smaller conference rooms to present more detailed information to teachers. A continual flow of 'hopeful staff' weaved in and out of these rooms to ask about living and working conditions.

The process was overwhelming. Hundreds of teachers from around the world hoped to get interviews with the top international schools. Naively we thought that our educational qualifications and experiences were an advantage. The reality was that the business side of international schools did not support the hiring of teachers whose salaries were going to be in the middle or at the top of their pay scales. Justifying the benefits of hiring experienced teachers over paying the lesser cost for teachers with only two years of experience was the never-ending challenge of school principals.

Our seniority and experience were disadvantages. Michael and I could be intimidating to new principals. In some cases, we knew more about the theories and methodologies to improve student learning than they did. In fact, all our international jobs were negotiated after the recruiting fairs, late in the season, except for the contracts we signed in Bangkok.

When Michael and I entered the convention hall on the first morning of the fair we noticed that many of the vacancies written on the lists behind the desks had already been crossed off. More surprising was that many of the vacancies from our database searches did not appear on the lists. Worse, neither of us had invitation cards for interviews in our file folders. We went in search of our representative for some answers.

Our representative told us that the lack of 'matches' was due either to teachers changing their minds at the last minute or the school administrators hiring teachers for those vacancies internally. He reassured us, saying that it was early and that new vacancies would appear as teachers moved sideways from school to school. He also suggested that we attend the social event organized that evening where we would have the opportunity to rub shoulders with the administrators and make a good impression. As we departed, I wondered how 'schmoozing' with administrators was going to make vacancies appear, but I didn't question his logic.

Michael and I checked our folders the next morning and thankfully we had an interview for a school in Vietnam. The interview went well, but the administrator was reluctant to offer us contracts. He told us that he would not commit before he interviewed teachers in England and the United States. His point of view was concerning. We had traveled to Bangkok confident that we would be offered contracts for the following year, but this man was not hiring. I had to wonder how many other schools had similar attitudes.

Our next interview was with the director of a school in Sudan. I did not like the director within minutes of meeting him, a very unusual reaction as I generally get along with people. A bully and a chauvinist, this director intentionally said things that put me on the defensive. The interview was unprofessional, and I had no desire to work for him. Michael agreed. The director's behaviour was typical of a person who felt the need to assert power over others — we had no desire to work for someone like that.

Later the same day, we had a quick interview with young administrators from Uzbekistan. There was a biology position for me, but they could not possibly hire Michael to teach computers as he had not taught it before. Even though he had been working with computer programs for years, in their minds he was not qualified to teach middle school students how to create Word documents and spread sheets.

At the end of the three-day International School Services (ISS) fair we had interviewed with two schools who did not offer contracts and one that we did not want to work for. Meanwhile, the younger teachers were getting multiple interviews and concrete offers to consider. We hoped that the second fair would provide more opportunities. Michael and I had to consider what we were going to do if we did not get a job.

Most of the schools at the second conference were the same. We received three interview invitations from schools that had not been at the ISS fair. We declined the request to interview with a school in Pakistan for fear of possible terrorist attacks. Even though the interview with a school in Qatar went well,

Michael was not hopeful as there were no concrete jobs at the school for either of us. The third opportunity was with the International School in Dhaka, Bangladesh. Bangladesh was definitely not on our list of potential places to teach, but at least the political situation there was better than in Pakistan. To learn more about the school we attended a video presentation and spoke with the middle year's program coordinator as well as a small group of teachers who were leaving the school. They all said positive things about working at the school as well as living in Bangladesh.

The interview with the International School of Dhaka went well and we were offered jobs within twenty-four hours. The job offers made us feel valued and re-established our faith in our credentials. In truth, we were disappointed with the search fair process. Even though there had been many suitable matches on the databases we had not been picked as first choices for interviews. After much discussion we concluded that a "bird in the hand was worth two in the bush." We accepted the offer to work at the International School of Dhaka (ISD).

The head of secondary was surprised by how quickly we said yes, but we needed work and there were no other opportunities. The largest recruiting fairs of the season had ended and the next one was in London, England. ISD's salary was acceptable, their International Baccalaureate (IB) curriculum was internationally renowned, and we had jobs in the areas that we wanted. What we did not realize at the time was what it was going to be like to live in one of the poorest and most densely populated countries in the world.

******

Gulshan buildings, power and water

When we moved to Bangladesh in August of 2009 the country had a population of 147 million people and they lived on less land than the United Kingdom. Our vacation to Cairo a year before had given us some exposure to the noise and crowds of densely populated cities, but the turmoil was tenfold. When we got off the plane in the capital city of Dhaka we were hit by a wave of heat and humidity as well as the smell and noise of a city of fourteen million people.

Michael and I were met at the baggage carousels by a member of the human resource team. By some miracle our luggage arrived, and we followed the driver to the school van. As we approached the parkade, I noticed an armed guard at the entrance. I thought this was odd, but quickly realized that his job was to keep beggars out. These beggars, mostly men, waited at the parkade entrance calling and gesturing hopefully for any gift of money. On the way to our apartment, I noticed that the roads were full of rickshaws, tuk-tuks, cars, and colorfully decorated trucks. In this chaotic jumble of humanity it was a challenge to drive without hitting something.

******

Most embassies and diplomatic clubs were in the northeast section of the sprawling city. Expatriate businessmen, NGO workers, and teachers from other schools lived in the residential areas called Gulshan I, Gulshan II, Banani, and Baridhara. The American School of Dhaka was in Baridhara while the International School of Dhaka was in a connecting neighborhood called Bushindhara.

Our new, large apartment in Gulshan I was on the third floor of a five-story building. The building was enclosed by a ten foot wall topped with barbed wire and broken glass. The ground floor was a parking lot for the residents and three guards took turns at the entrance gate twenty-four hours a day. These men cooked and slept in a small shelter at the back of the building.

Our Gulshan apartment had high ceilings and included three bedrooms, a living room, a dining room as well as a kitchen. Two of the bedrooms had ensuites and two tiny rooms designed for maids were located next to the kitchen. The floors were all tiled. Summers in Bangladesh were hot and humid with temperatures hovering around thirty degrees Celsius, so small air conditioning units were provided in the main bedroom and living room.

When we arrived, the rooms were sparsely furnished with two of the bedrooms having nothing in them at all. The living room had a couch, coffee table and a TV on a stand, while the dining area had a large table with six chairs, and a built-in display cabinet. Michael and I were not concerned by the lack of furniture. Within a few weeks our twelve cubic metre shipment of household items would arrive from Moscow.

Our new apartment had decorative bars on all the windows and the balconies were enclosed as well. In fact, all the buildings had bars on the windows and balconies. Initially I did not understand the need for these bars. The screens on the windows were not a hundred percent effective and mosquitoes got in. We slept under a mosquito net to prevent catching malaria or dengue fever.

During the day the street in front of our apartment was full of activity. Cars and rickshaw bicycles carried people and goods up and down the street. Transport rickshaws piled high with pots and pans and other light products passed by. Work gangs dug trenches and laid cables by hand, chanting songs as they laboured. My favorite sight was the men who walked by carrying baskets full of live chickens on their heads.

There was no large-scale garbage removal in our neighborhood. The job fell to a man who would ride by on a decrepit rusty bicycle with baskets hanging from the back wheel. The man would pick through the garbage and sort out anything that could be recycled. These items were placed in different baskets. The non-recyclable went into the larger middle bin. He did this for all the buildings on our street, an endless task that would have given him a few dollars a day in wages. Garbage was a resource that had value and street kids would collect plastic and paper in bags to sell to the recyclers at the end of the day.

*****

There was a plethora of wires and cables coiled around various poles, some dangling down to the sidewalks like wisteria. These nests of cables reminded me of the streets of Bangkok. We were told that companies would hang new cables as the technology improved, but would not bother to remove the old ones. Over the years mounds of coiled cables grew on the poles weaving into and out of buildings. It was common for locals to pirate cable and power services.

In Bangladesh thirty percent of the population lived on less than a dollar a day—a level of poverty difficult to imagine. Most of the uneducated youth were destined to be labourers in construction, seamstresses in the clothing industry, vendors in markets, and drivers for the rickshaw fleet, which transported most of the population. Street children picked up recyclable garbage, ran errands or became beggars. Any disability, either physical or mental, forced people to beg and live on the streets.

In our residential area, ghettos of tents and cardboard houses had built up around the reservoir lakes. Rickety outhouses perched precariously over the water added to the unhealthiness of the city. Some of the ghettos had been cleared away by the government, but the problem with housing and overcrowded apartments was systemic. There was little incentive for the government to modernize or create social programs to address poverty. Human labour was used for everything and if they modernized or industrialized many people would be out of work. In addition, there was an underlying level of corruption that was endemic and was just "the way things were." Owners got wealthy, and labourers toiled for a pittance.

It was amazing to see what groups of people can do without machines. Manual labourers carried baskets of sand, bricks, and other construction materials on their heads into and out of work sites. On the riverbanks ant-trains of workers unloaded ships from the brick factories as well as from the farms and factories located upriver. The resurfacing of the smaller roads was done by teams of men. Tar was heated in large barrels and then poured on the road in small batches and raked into place. It was a hot and smelly job.

Construction equipment like backhoes and cement trucks were rarely seen. Foundations and trenches for cables and water pipes for new buildings and maintenance were all dug by hand. Cement was mixed on site for smaller building projects. When we lived there kiln dried bricks were broken into pieces by older women on the sides of the street to create the gravel percentage needed for cement. In the second year we started to see small, mechanized crushers. I am not sure what the ladies did for money when they were made redundant.

Bamboo poles were used as scaffolding on most construction sites in Bangladesh. Foundation pilings were pounded in using the ancient technology of winches and a weight being guided by men clinging to a bamboo framework. Wall and ceiling forms were filled one by one with concrete mixed by barrel load and brought up by baskets on the heads of the workers. Labourers came from the country to live and work on building sites. Michael and I heard the labourers singing in the evenings and saw them huddling around small fires used to heat water and cook meals. The workers slept on mats and hung their few possessions on ropes in the sleeping area. Occasionally we saw metal scaffolding at building sites, but they were not the norm. Usually these buildings were being constructed by a foreign Non-Government Organization.

Adding to the general mayhem, building codes were often ignored and sometimes extra floors were added to the original plans. When I asked when a newly completed mall would open my driver told me that the builder had violated the codes and that it would not open until two floors were removed. The practice of building extra floors resulted in many buildings collapsing over the years; the most infamous occurred in 2013 when over 1100 women were killed when the Rana garment factory building collapsed. The death toll of the Rana collapse caused international outrage and building inspections increased to help prevent future collapses.

******

Dhaka was incredibly noisy. During the day car horns blared continually. Michael was sure that the horns were louder than in the west. At night large trucks and machines were allowed to drive on the streets to deliver materials to construction sites. The noise of construction deliveries drove some teaching colleagues to yell out their windows at two in the morning. In addition, international flights arrived and took off in the early morning hours and the flight path was directly above our neighborhood. We lived in a symphony of noise that went on twenty-four hours a day.

No one got anywhere quickly as traffic volume was well over the planned capacity. When there was a space in traffic drivers tended to go as fast as possible. Pedestrians had no rights and we needed to look in all directions before crossing the roads. When we traveled in the school vans, I could not look out the front window. I did not want to witness the endless near misses with pedestrians, rickshaws, buses and cars.

******

The tap water in Dhaka was not safe to drink. It was full of bacteria, which caused diarrhea and other gastrointestinal issues. We bought drinking water which was delivered on a weekly basis in large blue bottles. We used this water for all cooking. We washed our dishes in tap water, but rinsed them with boiling water to sterilize them. When we showered, we kept our mouths closed and we used bottled water to brush our teeth. There was no way of knowing if ice was made from clean water, so we never asked for ice at restaurants. Salads and other leafy vegetables could contain pathogenic microorganisms so they were off the menu.

In my second year I met one of the managers of the water treatment plant. She told me that Dhaka's water was pulled directly from the river and treated to produce western quality drinking water. She assured me that the water leaving the plant was tested and safe to drink. Unfortunately, by the time it came out of the apartment taps it was polluted. The system had not been designed to handle the density of the population and the fact that thousands of people lived in the streets. It was well known that the water mains and secondary pipes were not maintained and in many cases were cracked. The handling of sewage was not closed loop and open sewers and drains made Dhaka exceptionally smelly. Public toilets were rare and rickshaw drivers and manual labourers urinated in the ditches beside roads. The outhouses found in ghettos and on building sites added additional human waste into the soil and aquafer. The pathogen rich ground water leached into the water pipes.

Regardless of the quality we were lucky to have water in our taps whenever we wanted it. The water mains were routinely shut off during the day as there were not enough pumping stations to maintain the pressure to the whole system. Our building had a cistern on the roof filled with city water. It was used when the main supply was turned off. In contrast, our maid, Piare, did not have a cistern on the roof of her building and no water came out of the taps when the mains were turned off to her district. Millions of people in Dhaka had limited access to water.

******

Ongoing intestinal problems were a common topic of conversation around the faculty lunch tables. In some instances, colleagues required hospitalization. I was the sickest I had ever been with food poisoning after attending an outdoor wedding reception dinner. The knives and forks for the western guests were in glasses filled with water. I assumed that the water had been boiled so I used the fork and knife rather than my fingers. Michael used his fingers to eat rather than trust the cutlery. His decision was the correct one. At two in the morning I started to vomit violently, followed by severe diarrhea. Luckily my salmonella poisoning did not require IV treatment. I had to miss a day of work and I stayed close to the toilet for twenty-four hours.

Michael, who usually had a weaker stomach, was not affected at all. I did not make that mistake again. We could never let our guard down when it came to the safety of the water and food when living in Bangladesh.

******

Bangladesh did not generate a consistent supply of electricity. Power outages or "brown outs" occurred daily throughout the country. Predictably, the number of outages and their length was worse in the summer when air conditioning units were on full force. I distinctly remember when the lights went off the first time. The outage was startling as there was no weather event to cause it and I could not think of a reasonable explanation. Within minutes the men downstairs in the parking area started the building's generator and some of our lights came back on. The sounds of generators running added to the cornucopia of noise in Dhaka.

The building generator only supplied electricity to certain plugs in the apartment and this did not include the refrigerator. Refrigerators would keep things cold for days if the door was not opened. We did not put much in the freezer because of these power fluctuations.

The power outages were necessary because there were not enough power plants to supply the electrical demands of the growing city. Therefore electricity generated by coal and natural gas power plants was rationed, but not in a predictable fashion. We never knew when the power would go out, just that it would. Once they started, outages usually lasted an hour. They rarely lasted for two, at least in the upper-class neighborhoods.

The population of Bangladesh was used to having their power go off and on daily and there was little political pressure to fix the problem. When the lights went off during lessons the kids did not notice, they just continued with what they were doing knowing the school generator would start within minutes. I found this behaviour to be extraordinary—accepting what we would consider a hardship as normal.

Wealthy neighborhoods had fewer power diversions and not much thought was given to how the poor areas might be coping. Certain areas went without electricity for large parts of the day if they had electricity at all. I told my students that daily power outages did not occur in North America or Europe. I hoped that one day the government of Bangladesh would invest in a renewable power supply like solar and wind and not be tied to coal and gas.

******

Beggars and getting around

"Poverty is not only about income poverty, it is about the deprivation of economic and social rights, insecurity, discrimination, exclusion and powerlessness."

-Irene Khan, former Secretary-General of Amnesty
International, 2010-

Getting around Bangladesh was not for the faint of heart. Walking was possible, but had its hazards. The locals stared at foreigners they saw on the streets. We were warned about this behaviour at the job fair. Some teachers were quite annoyed by the staring and would yell at the crowd to stop. Their yelling did not fix the problem and caused even more people to turn and stare. I learned to ignore the behaviour as openly staring at strangers was obviously a cultural norm and not considered impolite.

Within the first month of our arrival, Michael and I went out for a few short walks to explore our neighborhood. Sidewalks existed on the side streets, but they were not level or a consistent width and usually service poles were placed in the middle of them. When not dodging poles, we walked around the many uncovered service holes and avoided the open sewage ditches.

To find out how we would tolerate walking in 30° C temperatures, Michael and I walked the ten blocks to the grocery store. We were on the main street where the sidewalks were better and noticed the Westin Hotel on the other side of the four-lane road. Outside the hotel's invisible perimeter, enforced by guards armed with sticks and guns, were groups of beggars.

On our first trip to the store Michael and I managed to ignore the small group of children who ran across the road to ask us for money. On our second trip we were literally swarmed by a group of adults as we walked back with our groceries. The crowd of beggars was so overwhelming and relentless that we retreated into a bank which had an armed guard.

We hoped that by going into the bank the group would disperse, but this did not happen. The beggars sat down and waited for us to come out. The guards inside the bank were disturbed by the behavior and after ten minutes they called a rickshaw so we could get away. Michael and I climbed into the rickshaw and our driver cycled off at top speed. The horde of beggars ran behind us for about a block before they finally gave up. After this unpleasant experience we always used the school vans provided for the teachers on a rota basis to buy groceries.

Rickshaws were the main means of transport for most of the population of Dhaka. Three wheeled bicycles with cozy seating for two. Rickshaws manoeuvred in and out of traffic—taking one could be faster than driving. Side streets were commonly used by rickshaws and other human powered vehicles. Large-wheeled trailers carrying heavy construction materials were pulled by teams of men. Bicycle rickshaws were adapted to transport a huge variety of materials. Flatbed bicycles were used for bricks and bamboo framing; box frames were used to transport buckets, baskets, and food sacks. The most interesting variation was a bicycle rickshaw designed to be a school bus. The eight to ten elementary age children sat in an enclosed cage with the driver pedaling in front.

The rickshaws designed to transport people had colourfully painted shade or rain covers which folded like accordions. Many of our friends used rickshaws to go to embassy clubs and some booked regular drivers. Our friend Chris supported his personal driver by paying for upgrades to the rickshaw as well as contributing to his children's schooling.

I did not like being pedaled around by another human being, so I only rode in rickshaws twice. The first was escaping from the beggars and the second was in Nepal as part of a tourist package. The wooden seats were not comfortable, and rickshaws would get stuck in traffic just like cars. Sitting in a rickshaw exposed foreign passengers to the same harassment from beggars as walking did.

Natural gas powered tuk-tuks were available for hire if you were willing to negotiate a price. After hearing some disturbing stories of foreigners being robbed by the drivers, we never got into one. The safest mode of transport was the school van system, and it was managed by the human resources department. Michael and I were assigned a specific day each week for a van and driver. We used our assigned van to go to the grocery stores, embassy clubs and restaurants in the Gulshan, Banini, and Baridhara areas. Before the holidays we would visit fair trade craft shops to buy gifts. Michael and I would coordinate with friends to double up on the ability to go out.

The volume of traffic in Dhaka was horrendous with cars and vans competing for space with hand pulled carts, rickshaws, tuk-tuks, and motorcycles. We did not get anywhere quickly. The occasional small herd of goats headed for the wet market added to the excitement. The length of time needed to drive anywhere made us stay within the area of the three connecting neighbor-hoods and the army golf club by the airport. We only traveled out of the city a handful of times.

Driving in the van was not necessarily a pleasant experience. At stoplights our conversations were interrupted by beggars tapping on the windows pleading for money. The behaviour was incessant and slightly disturbing. The driver would try to shoo them away because if one beggar got money our van would be swarmed by others. We witnessed this happen to drivers in cars. We had to pretend the beggars were not there and this was hard to do. Beggars were people in need, but they were organized by handlers who took a percentage, if not all of the money donated to them. Giving money to beggars did not solve the underlying problem of an inadequate social system servicing the increasing volume of people moving into Dhaka from country villages.

The Islamic faith promoted donations to those less fortunate as one of the Five Pillars of Islam. Entrances to mosques were lined with people begging. A family who lived on the bridge we crossed to go to work transported their disabled mother to the Mosques on a weekly basis.

Another time when the wealthy helped the not so fortunate was Eid Al-Adha, or the feast of sacrifice. In the weeks leading up to this holiday Muslims who could afford to would buy a sheep or goat to slaughter. The wealth of individuals was estimated by the number and type of animal purchased for the Eid Al-Adha holiday. Goats and sheep were purchased by the middle class, imported cattle and camels were purchased by the upper class. Brahman cattle were a favourite, and we saw many of them in our area. Camels were seen in front of the wealthiest families' houses.

A real-life menagerie, the animals were kept inside the housing compounds in the parking areas or in available spaces close to the owner's buildings. The ritual slaughtering was humane compared to some western slaughterhouse methods. On the specific day of slaughter, the animals were blessed and killed by trained religious men with sharp ceremonial knives. Once slaughtered the meat was distributed into three parts. The first went to the family, the second to friends and the third was given to the poor in a respectful manner. The poor walked to the wealthier areas. We witnessed hundreds of people carrying bags of butchered meat in our neighbourhood. Some teachers were upset about the slaughtering required by this religious ceremony. I found this a bit hypocritical. After all, the meat we eat is slaughtered and not necessarily as humanely.

******

Shopping for Food

Dhaka did not have large grocery stores when we lived there. Fruits and vegetables as well as general household products were sold at large covered markets. Meat was sold in separate wet markets which were 'spectacularly odoriferous' due to the heat. Because we did not speak Bangla the vendors took advantage of our ignorance, smiling as they did so. When Michael and I discovered that we were paying triple the local cost we were not pleased. We stopped going to the open markets and sent our maid Piare in our place. She took shopping for us very seriously and kept a tally of what she spent on each item. Piare was an excellent cook who made wonderful fruit salads, curries, and chapatti.

We had not wanted a maid, but there was an unwritten rule that new teachers adopted the contracts of the hired help of the leaving teachers. We were told by the hiring team that we would need a maid and Piare was available. It turned out that the particulate matter in the air of Dhaka was so high that our floors had to be washed every second day. As we left for work early and returned in the late afternoon, Michael and I did not regret hiring Piare to clean and cook for us.

******

In our district there were five stores which catered to expatriates. The stores were exclusive and armed security guards ensured that beggars and anyone who could not afford the prices stayed outside the parking areas. None of the stores were large and their supplies were limited. Michael and I bought sizeable quantities of our favourite items when they appeared on the shelves; it could be months before they would reappear.

Supply problems were especially acute for the Australian shop located in the Banini district. The official story was that the re-supply shipments were held up at customs waiting for the appropriate "fee" for release. When a shipment arrived word quickly spread among the expat community and the shelves emptied. Priority was given to getting there as soon as possible. Good toilet paper was worth the effort. We could buy toilet paper at the other stores, but it was not as soft. Michael and I discovered that the cheapest no-name toilet paper in Bangladesh had holes in it.

The Chinese-Asian grocery store in the Banini neighborhood was located on the second floor of an apartment block. They had limited stock, but they carried the sauces that Michael grew up with as well as the beans and noodles that I liked. We bought sticky rice and seaweed wrappers and made sushi for our friends. Occasionally we found frozen duck breasts which were a real treat.

It was not until our second year that we found beef which was edible. Our usual choices were chicken, pork, and goat, which for some reason the Bangladeshi called mutton. We did our weekly shopping at a small strip mall. There were two small western style grocery stores as well as other shops. One of these shops had a foreign-born butcher who was married to a Bangladeshi woman. The family owned a beef farm. With his help they were able to keep their cattle free of parasites. The meat of the healthy cattle was a huge improvement over the beef we had tried before.

******

"Medicine" was the euphemism for alcohol in Bangladesh. Alcohol was sold at specialized wholesale stores. The Australian teachers called them 'bottle shops'. The stores were located behind large secure gates and passports were required to gain entrance. Passport numbers were needed on verification forms when alcohol was purchased and, like in Russia, the selection on display was not necessarily what was available. Once the order had been recorded and foreign identification verified, we picked up the alcohol on the way out. The alcohol stores only accepted cash, which was just as well as we did not trust them with our visa card numbers.

Michael and I usually bought alcohol on Saturdays when we had the school van. If we wanted to buy wine during the week Michael had to leave school early to get there before they closed. In these instances, he used Chris's rickshaw driver. On the way to the store Michael carried enough money to support a ghetto family for three months. And it bought three bottles of wine! We were privileged westerners.

******

What to do in Dhaka

Michael and I did not belong to an embassy club like many of our teacher friends. The Canadian embassy had a complicated process to join if you were not an embassy employee or diplomat. Michael and I did not bother trying as we were allowed to join our friends as guests at the Australian club and Dutch club on weekends. Non-members could enjoy their restaurant services, but could not play tennis or squash.

If we did not feel like eating at a club there were a variety of international restaurants to choose from. The Korean restaurant had hotplates in the centre of the tables. Something that I had not seen before. We managed not to burn ourselves while we cooked the traditional dishes. Their beef bulgogi reminded me of the Korean booth at the Anglo-American School during Moscow's International day. The Chinese restaurant's food was genuine and tasty. The English menu had translation errors similar to the one in Moscow, which made us chuckle.

A favourite of our group of friends was a fancy Indian restaurant. The front gate was very ornate with carved doors and lighting that produced an "Aladdin" feel. There was a small herd of local deer in the front yard, so the building was surrounded by a high wall. The food was excellent. They offered a good wine selection, so we always went there to celebrate birthdays.

There really was not much to do during the week other than shop for food and crafts so Michael and I began inviting friends over to eat homemade sushi and play scrabble. Heather quickly learned all our scrabble tricks and, much to our chagrin, she became unbeatable. Playing scrabble in the evenings became a common pastime and everyone in our group took turns hosting and making dinner.

******

Golf

A group of teachers at the school played golf and had their own clubs. We collaborated, and using the weekend vans, we managed to play at least twice a month. Extreme temperatures and torrential rain were the only things that interfered with our plans. The nine-hole Army course was located close to our housing districts, and it was a good course for beginners. The second course in Dhaka, called Kurmitola, had eighteen holes. Kurmitola was designed for golfers who played a lot and had established handicaps. There was a club house and the green fees were higher than the Army course. Most of our group were beginner golfers, so the Army course suited us better.

The Army course was busy, and we had to wait to tee off. Caddies and ball boys were provided as part of the fee to play. It was crowded on the first tee with four players, four caddies, and four ball boys. As the first player got ready to tee off, the ball boys would run to where they thought they were going to hit the ball.

I found it difficult to hit the ball towards someone. Luckily, the ball boys were good at leaping out of the way if we hit it further than they thought. The course had fruit trees and our caddies would pick the fruit for us when it was ripe. We sampled fresh lychee and other exotic tropical fruits like palm nuts.

When Michael hit into the woods the ball miraculously appeared on the side of the fairway. The "ball boy bounce" was the friend of beginner golfers. Heather and Linda would find their balls on "tufts" of grass so that they had a better chance of hitting a good shot. There was a pond on the left side of the second hole which Heather loved to hit towards. The ball boys learned to stand in front of the pond to stop the rolling ball from going in and we witnessed some pretty dramatic saves. There were a lot of water hazards on the course and used balls could be bought in bulk. They were sold by the ball boys who retrieved them from the ponds at the end of the day.

The grounds keeper used few machines other than grass cutters. Groups of men and women weeded fairways by hand with wide brim hats on their heads protecting them from the sun. Coring or aeration of the greens was done with a large hand tool resembling a spade. Once a year teams of men aerated all the greens within a day with little impact on play. Sand was spread onto the green with the excess removed by hand. The whole procedure was very impressive.

The Army course was a relaxed and fun place to play. Fees were paid at a booth and snacks were purchased from a man sitting behind a fold out table. The ambience changed when the club house was completed. The green fees increased and the men were told that they had to wear long pants with belts. A new pro shop was filled with clothing and clubs. The expectation was that players would look the part of professionals. Our group was not impressed with the change in dress code and we did not golf as often after the price went up.

******

Brass village

Michael and I organized a day trip to the brass village during one of our holidays. The brass village was in Dhamrai, a two-hour drive northwest of Dhaka and listed on a tourist site as one of the things to do when visiting Dhaka. The final destination was an old colonial house which had seen better days.

There was a central courtyard surrounded by the main house and out-buildings. The owner of the house greeted us at the gate. His family were traditional brass workers who made brass statues and other artifacts using the lost-wax method. There were very few people capable of this traditional method of metal work. Intricate brass figurines and statues were first carved from wax by the artisans. A mold of clay was formed around the wax figure. The clay-wax combination was fired in a kiln and in the process the wax would melt and flow out a specially placed hole. Once cooled the empty clay mold was filled with liquid brass. When the brass cooled the clay was removed and the brass figurine or statue would emerge. Each mold only made one brass figure which was then sanded and polished. Though they made many items, no two products were the same. Michael and I purchased an intricately carved fish as well as an elephant. Both were hollow with doors for tea candles.

******

For one holiday we joined three friends on a trip to the Bandarbans hill tracts close to the Myanmar border. After flying to Chittagong, the five of us were driven to the resort in an air-conditioned van. Our itinerary included a drive to the highest point in Bangladesh where we could see the border with Myanmar. The people who lived in the area were not Bangla speakers and they had strong ties to the Myanmar tribes that were being persecuted at the time. A large refugee camp was nearby. A strong military presence with checkpoints along the roads dissuaded more refugees from coming into Bangladesh.

Over the next few days, we visited a pineapple plantation, a Buddhist temple, and small villages to look at local crafts. We were taken to a small waterfall and lake where a large goat caused trouble in the parking lot. The goat was cute until it tried to butt us as we climbed out of the van. The holiday was an escape from the noisy city. The Bandarbans offered views of green hills in a less densely populated region of the country.

******

Bangladesh had two main seasons; it was either hot and raining or hot and dry. From April to October, it rained torrentially every day. The heavy rain was predictable and lasted about an hour. Everyone outside got wet, but the rain was warm and wet clothes dried quickly. Large puddles were left behind. A teaching colleague innocently rode her bicycle into what she thought was a shallow puddle. It turned out to be a large hole that swallowed her and her bicycle completely. It was a scary event as she was at high risk of being exposed to cholera and other nasty bacteria. The water was well mixed with the local feces from the open sewers and outhouses. From that day forward, she avoided puddles.

When the tall grasses flowered in October it was a sign that the dry season had arrived, bringing with it relatively cooler weather. It would not rain again until March. The kilns that made bricks would start up at this time. There were thousands of these kilns surrounding Dhaka and they belched black smoke from their tall smokestacks. I am not sure which was worse, torrential rain and mosquitoes or breathing air that was full of smoke and particulate matter.

******

Fifteen minutes of fame

Michael and I both experienced our fifteen minutes of fame while living in Dhaka. A friend in the IT department at school knew someone who made films in Dhaka. At one point we were asked if we would be interested in being "extras" for one of these short films. Our friend promised it would be a hassle-free adventure. We were not enthusiastic; Michael and I had become distrustful of the intent of some of the events we were asked to attend. The filmmaker most likely wanted foreign faces in the background, but did not want to say as much. After being asked a few times, we realized that the request was not going to disappear. To maintain good relations, we agreed to participate.

On the morning of the filming, I woke up with a swollen right eye caused by a sinus infection. I was feeling pretty miserable and we tried to beg off our commitment when our friend and the filmmaker arrived to pick us up. Not easily flustered, the film maker told us we were the only people who could do our roles and that my swollen eye would be covered by makeup. With no excuse good enough, we climbed into the car on the understanding that we would stop at a pharmacy to get some antibiotics. Unlike in Canada, antibiotics were easily purchased over the counter in Bangladesh, Thailand, and the UAE.

Michael and I asked questions about the film's story as we crawled through the usual Dhaka traffic jams. The filmmaker explained that it was a small film about Bangladesh and asked if we would be willing to speak a few lines. The request came as a bit of a shock—we were not actors and had never aspired to be actors. He reassured us, saying we would be great. We assumed the film was a university project and would not be seen by a large audience, so we agreed to speak a few lines of dialogue.

We finally arrived at a university complex and entered a building with a stage and theatre seating. It looked very professional with spotlights and other lighting set at specific angles. I saw three static cameras as well as one on a rail system manned by camera personnel. Forty to fifty extras were sitting in the seats and the actors were standing on the side of the stage. There was a podium on the left of the stage which was decorated to look like an awards or graduation ceremony. Michael agreed to be a reporter in the audience and was taken off to be prepped. His task was to ask the main actor, who we found out later was quite famous in Bangladesh, two questions.

I was instructed to stand behind the podium and say one line which introduced the main character. While make-up was applied to my swollen eye, I frantically practiced my one line. I had never done anything like it before and I was very nervous. I spoke confidently to students all day, but to say one line in front of a camera was not the same. I needed to concentrate to say my line in a normal speaking voice. The experience gave me a new appreciation of actors and the skill needed to remember dialogue. Once I introduced him in English the actor spoke his lines in Bangla. I had no idea what he was saying.

Michael and I fuddled through the filming without too much difficulty as everyone was supportive. Multiple takes were needed for the final product. We finished the day doing secondary recordings of our lines to overdub the original soundtrack. What we had thought would be a few hours took all day. Regardless of the time spent, Michael and I were treated well, and we enjoyed working with the cast and crew. At the end of the shoot we were driven home and thanked profusely by the film maker.

Three months later my grade six students told me they had seen me on TV. It took me a moment to remember our filming experience at the university. My students told me that Michael and I had been involved in the making of a television advertisement to promote Bangla as the national language of Bangladesh. The advertisement ran for months on the local TV stations and was seen by millions of people. Not a small film piece as we had originally assumed. Michael stored a copy in our Bangladesh photo and video archives to show to our grandchildren.

******

Visitors

Emily, a teaching friend from Moscow, came to see us when we lived in Bangladesh. Entry visas were required for most nationalities, but Americans could buy their visas on arrival. Unfortunately, when Emily arrived the visa officer would not accept the Euros she was carrying; they wanted US dollars or Taka, the Bangladesh currency. She was directed to go to the ATM to get out US dollars. Emily could not see an ATM machine in the secure area, so she walked to the bank machine in the unsecure area, extracted money, and walked back into the secure area to buy the visa.

Proceeding through passport control without any further problems, Emily met us at the baggage collection area. Michael and I found it amazing that she had been allowed to wander between the secure and unsecure areas without question. Regardless of the bizarre and inconsistent nature of this event, we were very happy that she had not been deported.

We arranged a boat trip to a weaving village the next day with our usual group of friends. We were picked up by the school van and driven to a pedestrian ferry crossing on the bank of a large river. People lined up to get into one of the many small flat boats. Each held ten to fifteen people. There were no seats, and passengers crouched on the bottom of the boats. Like Venetian gondolas the boat ferries were paddled back and forth in a continuous stream by men who stood at the back of each boat using large paddles.

Our presence attracted attention and a group of Bangladeshi men stopped what they were doing to watch us walk towards our tour boat. There was no official dock, so the flat bottom boat had pulled up as close to the shore as it was able. A twelve-inch (30 cm) plank was lowered for us to walk up. Fortunately, we were all fit enough to balance on the plank. Once we were on board the boat slowly motored up the river to the weaving village. We disembarked down the same small wooden plank to an audience of village children.

The weaving village was not part of the large-scale fashion industry. Barefoot children were scantily dressed in second-hand clothing. Houses were built from corrugated tin panels and wood. The streets were well trodden dirt. The tour organizer took us into small houses where women wove intricate filigree patterns on wooden looms. After the tour we were taken to the small outdoor shop with the unspoken understanding that we would buy a scarf or sari before getting back on the boat. Most of us complied, hoping that the money would be used to improve the conditions of the families living there.

The scenic boat trip wound through pastoral farms where farmers used centuries-old practices. Fields were small, and harvesting was done using hand held sickles not machines. We also saw evidence of the millions of dollars of aid that had been given to Bangladesh over the years for infrastructure projects. At one point, the boat went under a huge new bridge that was finished, but it did not have roads on either side of it. A bridge in the middle of nowhere, built using international money for a purpose that had got lost along the way. Emily only stayed for a few days. In this time she experienced the outrageous traffic, noise, smell, and human population density that constituted our life in Dhaka.

******

In the same year, my friends Ann and Lyn from British Columbia added Bangladesh to their Indian tour. I arranged a trip to Sonargaon, a historical site close to town. We visited the newly finished Folk Arts Museum before entering the historic park site. The gardens were laid out like European estates and very beautiful.

For some reason, maybe the fact that we were foreign, other visitors to the park thought we were movie stars. At first, people took our pictures without our permission. After a while we were asked to be included in family pictures. Initially we agreed to these requests, but the crowds started getting bigger and we got concerned for our safety. When mothers started asking us to hold their babies for good luck, we made a hasty retreat to the van and drove home. We had a brief glimpse into what people in the public spotlight cope with every day.

During her visit Ann had a distressing encounter with a bank machine. I had forgotten to warn her that the Bangladesh ATM machine money slot doors shut faster than the machines in Canada. When she went to make a withdrawal from the machine, she did not take her cash quickly enough and the money retracted and the door closed. After a panicked phone call to Canada, Ann was assured by her bank that their records would have recorded that she had not taken the money. We continued to use bank machines, but learned to grab our money as soon it appeared.

Ann and Lyn were amazed by the sheer number of rickshaws on the streets. They discovered that most rickshaw drivers were paid a percentage of their daily takings—they did not own the bicycle they rode. Lyn heard about an organization that was committed to helping drivers buy rickshaws. She joined the fund-raising campaign on her return to Canada. Unfortunately, like many other charities that started off with good intentions, this one became a bit suspect. We were not sure how much of the money went to purchasing rickshaws and how much went to the organizers. The lack of transparency led Lyn to cease her fund-raising campaign.

******

Bangladeshis decorated their houses or apartment buildings with fairy lights and banners when their daughters got engaged. When we arrived in August our apartment building was covered with these festive fairy lights. It was enchanting. Most weddings were held from August to October when the long grass bloomed and the weather was cooler.

During Ann's and Lyn's visit we attended a Bangladeshi wedding that I had been invited to. When we arrived at the hall, we were taken to chairs covered in red velvet and gold brocade located at the front of the room. I do not know why we were put in these places of honor; the groom and I were only acquaintances. Before sitting down, we said hello to the bride who was in a separate room. Wearing the traditional wedding sari and draped in jewelry she sat on a decorated bed waiting for the groom's entourage to arrive.

When the groom arrived, he was led to a decorated tent where he put on new clothes provided by the bride's family. The traditional wedding ceremony was very elaborate. At one point the bride walked around the chair where her husband sat three times and then washed his feet. The action reflected the subservient nature of the woman's role in traditional society—a custom that would hopefully change. The bride was well educated, and her income matched her new husband's.

The large banquet hall had tables set for the catered dinner. Ann, Lyn and I were ushered to one of the tables and plates of delicious curries were brought out to us. As we sat back after eating, I noticed people standing at the sides of the hall. They were waiting to sit down. I realized we were expected to leave so newly arriving guests could enjoy the banquet. Traditional weddings were day long events and hundreds of people were invited. We had the privilege of seeing the ceremony as well as eating while others only came to the banquet. All guests brought presents of money or household appliances and the mountain of boxes at the front door grew.

******

Tyler, another lifelong friend from the Anglo-American School of Moscow visited from the Philippines in November of 2010. To avoid the issue that we had with Emily's visa purchase, Michael researched the exact cost of the visa so that Tyler brought the correct amount in US dollars. Unbeknownst to us the cost rose from $50.00 USD to $100.00 USD the day Tyler flew in.

When Tyler did not appear in the baggage area Michael saw him in the holding area through the new Plexiglas barrier. They were able to communicate that he was ten dollars short of the hundred required for the visa. The ATM machine in the holding area was not working and when Michael tried the ATM on his side of the barrier it also did not work. To get the required US dollars Michael had to return to our house to get it from our USD cash reserve. After driving back to the airport Michael crumpled the money up into a ball and threw it to Tyler over the top of the barrier. A little unorthodox, but it worked. With the visa issue sorted Tyler proceeded through passport control.

While he was visiting, Tyler told us about a tragic accident that had occurred on a school trip in the Philippines. The tour company had changed the travel itinerary and presented the students with an opportunity to swim in some pools just up from a waterfall. The students had been told not to go towards the waterfalls. There were various versions of what happened in the newspapers, but what was known was that two boys were swept away and tragically drowned in a matter of minutes.

The teachers on the trip, regardless of where they were during the accident, were all named in a lawsuit launched by one of the mothers. She was looking for compensation for her personal loss from the school—a common practice with proceedings that could go on for years. Because they were named in the lawsuit the teachers on the trip would most likely be arrested and placed in jail for an indefinite amount of time. Philippine jails were not nice places and prisoners relied on relatives to feed and clothe them. The school encouraged the teachers involved to leave the country to avoid this scenario. A prudent strategy as, according to the *Philippine Sun Star* it took five years for a settlement to be reached between the parents and the school.

Two years after Tyler told us this story Michael and I were asked to take a group of students on a kayaking trip by a young enthusiastic athletics coordinator. The first words out of our mouths were "do they know how to swim"? When he answered that he didn't know, we were shocked. Clearly, he did not understand the risks associated with water and children.

The athletics coordinator was confused by our negativity as there had been no issues the year before. We asked that the students be surveyed to see if they could swim, and the results confirmed our fears. Six of the students could not swim at all. These non-swimming students were going to be sleeping in floating cabins with floating walkways that did not have handrails. Tripping and falling off the walkway on the way to the toilet was a distinct possibility. The risk of drowning went to the top of the list of things to be avoided.

Michael and I requested to go on the grade eleven and twelve service trips to the north to avoid the worry. Our request was accepted by the coordinator. He then reflected on our concerns about drowning and made sure that the students took swimming lessons as part of their PE curriculum before leaving on the trip. The requirement ensured that the non-swimmers could at least float if they fell in the water. The trips itinerary was changed to have more hiking than kayaking and there were no accidents.

******

Bali, Nepal, India and Bhutan

When we worked in Bangladesh, Michael and I flew to Nepal, Bali, India, and Bhutan for school holidays. Our international flights home to Canada linked through Hong Kong or Beijing. Flights left early in the morning and unpredictable traffic made it stressful to get to the airport. We left hours before our departure time to ensure that the van got to the airport with time to spare. Once through security we people watched.

It was obvious that many of the departing male passengers had never been on a plane before and most were wearing their first "foreign" clothes. Price tags hung from shirt collars and new shoes were worn without socks. These young men were on their way to the Middle East to build the skyscrapers of Dubai and Abu Dhabi or work in one of the blue-collar systems that supported commercial business and tourism.

Construction companies recruited young men by offering salaries higher than the dollar a day they got carrying sand off barges at home. On arrival in the UAE their passports would be taken away and they were housed in trailers within compounds. High density made these compounds rife with disease before the Covid-19 pandemic. Buses provided by the owners would transport men to and from the construction site. Construction workers worked long hours under gruelling conditions, and many died from accidents. The owners provided an annual trip home, but there was little else to make the men's life easier. I had not been aware of this form of human exploitation before working in Bangladesh.

The hotel conglomerates were one step up from the construction industry. They employed men and women from all over Asia and the world to serve the booming tourist and

123

convention industries. Waiters, cleaners, and cooks all needed to be imported. In most cases, they were paid better than in their home countries, but salaries were still pitiful.

Taxis and buses employed tens of thousands of men. We chatted to one taxi driver from Bangladesh who was so pleased that he was sharing a local villa with 'only' fifteen other taxi drivers. These men thought they were moving up in the world and were thankful for the opportunity to make and save money. From our perspective they were living a life of indentured servitude.

******

Nepal was an amazingly beautiful country, and we went there twice. On our first holiday to Nepal, Michael and I flew to Pokhara via Kathmandu. We went to Pokhara because of the Fulbari resort hotel, which advertised a golf course and relaxing massages. Both were on the list of things we wanted to do. Also, Pokhara was the gateway to the breath-takingly stunning Annapurna Mountain range.

The connecting plane to Pokhara was a prop plane just big enough to carry our golf bags and carry-ons. The airport was tiny and our luggage was hand carried from the plane to a bench inside the one-room terminal building. Even though the airport was only one room it still had segregated security lines for men and women just like the Kathmandu airport.

Outside the Pokhara airport we found the Fulbari hotel driver holding a sign with our names. Once greeted, we were asked to place our bags into a beat up van. In 2009, the Fulbari was listed as a five-star hotel on the internet. As is true for many things in the developing world, never trust what is advertised. At least half of the hotel complex needed serious repairs because of long term water damage and mold.

Regardless of the overall state of the hotel our rooms and the dining area were world class. From our room we could see the spectacular "Fishtail" or Machapuchare in the distance. One of the tallest mountains in the Annapurna range and significantly higher than the surrounding mountains, its peak was covered by snow. Considered sacred by the Nepalese no climbing permits have ever been granted. It remains the highest unclimbed mountain on Earth.

Michael and I were excited to try the golf course. The name "Yeti" was written on a dilapidated sign on the path to the first hole. The golf shop had a few items of clothing, golf balls and tees for sale. We arranged for tee times for the next three days though the booking pages were blank.

Our fee included caddies who were teenagers. Neither of them had any knowledge of golf, but they were friendly and willing to carry our bags. As we walked to the first tee, Michael and I could see that the course was in a sorry state. The grass was ankle deep in places. Our caddies told us that the cutting machines were broken.

As long as we stayed on the fairway the course was playable. The mountains were breathtaking and the river below us formed deep ravines. The second hole had men hitting 140 yards over a ravine that was at least a kilometre deep. The women's tee was closer to the hole and did not have the ravine as a hazard.

Undaunted, Michael hit ball after ball into the ravine until he finally hit one well enough to land on the green. We all cheered and walked around the ravine to the green. On the green there were no railings to prevent us from going over the edge. Safety did not seem to be a priority for the greens keepers.

On the second day the course professional joined us. He was excited to play with someone and talked about his achievements in the regional golf tournaments. On the second hole he exhibited no fear as he chipped his ball while standing less than three feet from the edge of the cliff. Every hole had unforgettable views of the Himalayan Mountain range. Playing the Yeti golf course was a once in a lifetime experience.

After three days of golfing, eating well, and enjoying relaxing massages we flew to Kathmandu. Michael had booked a tour company to show us the city. After fighting our way through the aggressive touts at the airport we managed to find our personal guide. Over the next few days, we traveled exclusively with this pleasant young man who was extremely knowledgeable about the history of Kathmandu and the heritage sites included in our personalized tour.

Our daily routine included being picked up in the morning, going to a temple, having lunch, and then going to a second temple before returning to the hotel. In the evenings Michael and I walked to the Thamel Market—a tourist area filled with shops and vendors selling trekking gear, music, handicrafts, souvenirs, woolen items, and clothing. Small grocery stores were located on street corners, as well as trendy coffee shops and restaurants. Pedestrians of all ages and ethnicities filled the narrow streets. The shop inventories catered to western tourists. I successfully resisted the temptation to buy a Turkish carpet. My desire to buy beautiful textiles was satisfied with the purchase of two woven pillow covers that would easily fit into my luggage.

*****

Nepal was a few steps up the economic ladder from Bangladesh though Kathmandu was a chaotic menagerie, possibly worse than Dhaka. In addition to the usual rickshaws and tuk-tuks, cows and water buffalo wandered the streets. The presence of these animals made it hard for the other modes of transportation to manoeuvre through the narrow streets, which had not been designed for the volume of traffic. Buddhism permeated the culture with calmness, and we found Kathmandu a pleasant city to visit.

The second time Michael and I went to Nepal we flew in from Bhutan. We were only there for three days and stayed at the Gokarna golf resort on the outskirts of Kathmandu. Located within a forest reserve and surrounded by nature, Gokarna was advertised as one of South Asia's most spectacular courses. When Michael and I played the course, troops of monkeys were sitting on most fairways. The monkeys would usually ignore our balls, but on one hole a monkey picked up Michael's ball and dropped it further down the fairway. After golfing, the resort offered fine dining and spa treatments in which we were happy to indulge.

Our second trip to Nepal was initiated by the fact that India would not issue us visas to enter India from Bhutan. We had purchased a multi-entry visa for a trip to Delhi at Christmas, but the Indian government required at least two months between border crossings. The spring holiday dates did not meet the criteria, so we traveled to Kathmandu rather than Darjeeling as we had originally planned.

******

Michael and I flew from Dhaka to Bali for the 2009-2010 Christmas holidays. We traveled via Kuala Lumpur and planned to spend a few days seeing the sites of the Indonesian capital on the return trip. In Bali we booked a small hotel north of the capital city. The hotel suite was funky with an outside shower, a feature that only worked in a warm climate. The only room that was completely sealed from the outside was the bedroom and it was air conditioned. The living and dining areas had walls which were not joined to the roof. We were concerned our personal possessions could be stolen and didn't leave anything of value behind when we went out.

We had heard some stories about using ATM bank machines in Bali and thought exchanging US dollars would be safer. At the exchange booth, the man dramatically counted the money in front of us twice. Michael was a bit suspicious so counted it for a third time after stepping away from the booth to discover that there was money missing from the agreed upon amount. We confronted the man who immediately gave us the "misplaced" amount with no apology. I am positive that the sleight of hand trick he used was very profitable with the less vigilant tourists. A similar sleight of hand trick had occurred at a Moscow money exchanger, and was why Michael had recounted the sum a third time.

We golfed in Bali on a few of its many courses. The courses we played had views of either the ocean or mountains. Designed for tourists, caddies and carts were included in the price. On a day off from golfing, Michael rented a motorcycle. We set off in the morning and drove to Ubud the artistic and spiritual center of Bali. Driving was relatively easy, and gas could be bought from kiosks at the side of the road in old two-litre water bottles. In Ubud we window shopped and found a place to eat lunch. On the return trip we stopped at the popular Monkey Forest. The grey long-tailed macaques were very aggressive and waited for opportunities to steal food and other items from people. I was not that keen on the monkeys, so we did not stay long.

At the Bali airport we walked to the departure gate and saw engine pieces on the pavement underneath the plane we were supposed to take. A mechanic was literally standing in the space where the engine should have been. We enthusiastically accepted the airline company's offer of a hotel for the night while we waited for a replacement plane. A German tour group was not happy with the delay. They were yelling and demanding something that was not possible. Michael and I retreated to the hotel pool and enjoyed another day on the island. A larger replacement plane allowed most stranded passengers to travel to Kuala Lumpur the next day.

******

In 2010 Michael and I went to India for the Christmas holidays. We planned an ambitious private tour through Rajasthan with stops in Agra, Jaipur, Jodhpur, Pushkar, and Delhi. My father, who had grown up in India and Chinese Turkestan until the age of twelve, decided to join us. My mother had no desire to see India and she visited her sister and brother-in-law in Australia instead.

My father had dual Canadian and British citizenship and Bangladesh offered a visa on arrival for British citizens, but India did not. He downloaded the forms for the Indian visa, filled them out and collected a money order for the specified fee from his bank. When he went to the Indian embassy to get everything processed the teller told him the money order was not for the correct amount and they could not accept it.

My father asked when the fee had been changed as he had followed the instructions on the application form very carefully. The clerk apologized and said it was just a recent change which had not been updated on the website. When he asked what the new fee was the difference was fifty cents less. He asked the teller if they could "keep the change," but this was not an option. My father had to get a new money order from the bank which was time consuming.

Michael and I were not surprised by the inaccuracies of the Indian website, and we had our own visa issues preparing for the trip. As we were technically residents of Bangladesh, we had to use a new on-line application system to apply for an Indian tourist visa. Michael completed the online forms and was assigned a number which correlated with a specific date and time to visit the Indian Embassy in Dhaka to have the visas put into our passports. He printed the forms because hardcopies were needed to accompany our passports when we went to the embassy.

Michael applied for the visas months in advance. When getting the forms and passports ready to go to the embassy, I noticed a box that asked for a second passport number if you held dual citizenship. Michael and I debated what to do as I had a British passport. We decided to be honest and I filled in my British passport number by hand naively thinking it would be a quick computer fix at the embassy.

The head of our school's human resources volunteered to go to the Indian Embassy with our passports and forms—he knew the system. He came back with bad news. Michael's visa had been processed without issue, but because my form did not match exactly the online one, mine could not be processed. We needed to fill in a new online form correctly and book a new appointment time. Meanwhile they would hold both our passports in the processing pile.

Getting an online form and time slot was not as easy the second time. The number of visa applications was limited. India opened batches of visas for Bangladeshi residents according to a schedule which was not published. When the booking spots were all taken you had to wait until the next batch was opened. No one could tell us when that would be. Michael spent days staying up until midnight waiting for new slots to open. When he finally did get access to a time slot it was two days before our

December departure date. Michael and I took time off work and went to the Indian Embassy personally to ensure that all went smoothly.

We waited in a room that needed a good coat of paint, but once we were in front of the passport clerk it only took a few minutes for him to stamp and process my visa. He returned Michael's already processed passport and we were ready to leave for our winter holiday in India.

My father joined us in Bangladesh a week before our winter break started. He had no issues getting his visa on arrival at the Dhaka airport as we were well practiced by this point. Michael and I left him to explore on his own while we worked. He walked to some of the local markets during the day and managed to avoid the beggars. In the evenings we went to our favourite restaurants and played scrabble with our usual group of friends.

On the weekend we managed a golf game at the Army course where my father wowed our friends with his superior golf skills. Dhaka reminded him of when we lived in Gulu, Uganda (1964-66). The level of poverty was comparable, but the culture and languages were different. He had hoped to be able to speak Urdu, a language he learned in India as a child, but the population of Bangladesh spoke Bangla and most of the population around Delhi spoke Hindi. My father did comment on the fact that his memory of Urdu returned when he heard smatterings of it spoken in the markets around Pushkar.

Michael and I organized a private van tour for our Indian holiday. The trip included traveling to the main cities of the province of Rajasthan to visit temples and palaces. We had no desire to drag luggage, which included golf bags, through crowded train or bus stations. The tour package included a private van with driver and a personal tour guide at each city. We were picked up from our hotel in the mornings and the guides accompanied us during the day. At temples and palaces they recited prepared speeches detailing the history and importance of the location. As a bonus the presence of a guide kept the beggars and touts away and their general knowledge of the historical sites was extensive.

Delhi, a city of twenty-one million, was more polluted than Dhaka. Rickshaws had been replaced by CNG tuk-tuks and there were more cars. The air pollution was so terrible that visibility was less than two hundred metres. Diesel power plants, agricultural burning and traffic exhaust were the largest contributors to the toxic chemical smog. Winter weather did not improve the situation as people used open wood fires for warmth and coal cooking fires.

Our first stop was the city of Agra. The day was clear and sunny, and the Taj Mahal was stunning. There were large crowds, but everyone patiently took turns sitting on the famous bench for the classic picture. We continued to Jaipur where we played golf and took in the historical sites.

We succumbed to the temptation of the carpet store in Jodhpur. My father bought three handmade carpets to replace ones which dated back to the 1950s and 60s. These were successfully shipped to Canada. I loved carpets, but Michael and I had two hand-made carpets which we bought in Russia and Cambodia. We did not really need another one and shipping anything to Bangladesh was risky.

We booked a five-star hotel for our stay in Jodhpur. We were staying there December 24th and 25th. We knew from past experience that hotels charged a set fee for Christmas dinner despite whether guests ate the meal or not. Five stars guaranteed that the food choices would be varied and of high quality. During the feast we were entertained by a band playing traditional instruments, a fire breathing juggler, and a woman who danced and balanced pots on her head. We ate outside with lighting provided by candles and carefully placed spotlights. It was a memorable evening as the food was exceptional.

The tour company booked a train for us to return to Delhi from Pushkar. Michael and I were concerned that the train would not run. At the time, protesters were threatening to blockade train tracks including the intercity rails lines. We were on a tight schedule, so we negotiated with the tour company to use the van to get us back to Delhi even though it was a very long drive. It was the right decision. On the day that we were scheduled to take the train the protestors blocked the tracks.

******

Haircuts

Language barriers and cultural differences made haircuts a challenge in most of the countries we lived in. In Moscow a male friend accidentally received a very short haircut because he unintentionally asked for a number two razor cut due to his poor Russian. To ensure this did not happen to him Michael asked a Russian speaking friend to accompany him to the barber. The barber shop was behind an unmarked door in a basement corridor inside a residential building. There were no sinks and a spray bottle of water was used to wet Michael's hair before it was cut. He did not see the scissors and combs being cleaned between customers. Luckily he did not get lice. The cost for the haircut was minimal, but there were only two choices for styles, the universal razor cut of different lengths or one which was slightly longer on the top.

Before Smart phones and translation apps communication with hairstylists was problematic. The typical Russian style for working women required blow drying and hair spray. To avoid the extra time required in the morning to do this, I let my hair grow until we traveled to Europe or returned to Canada.

I used off-the-shelf box brands to color my hair in Canada, but in Moscow the choices for boxed hair dyes were red, auburn, black or bleached blond. Light brown was not a culturally popular color. The auburn dyes I tried turned my hair various shades of red or purple. I resorted to buying a year's worth of brown hair color kits during the summer holidays abroad and carried them in my luggage back to Moscow. Airport security never questioned me about the hair dye, toothpaste, and coffee beans I packed in my bags.

In Bangladesh most women had long black hair, so salons concentrated on preventing hair fall. There was a plethora of products for thickening hair and preventing hair fall which we did not know about in the west. A freelance expat hairstylist cut most of my friend's hair. I joined her list of clients. Trained in the UK, she had access to the dyes and tints requested by her European clientele, so I no longer packed them in my suitcase. Originally from New Zealand she was a fabulous hair stylist and would come to our apartment with her equipment. Having my hair cut at home reminded me of the time I lived on a boat on Hornby Island. The local haircutter would bring a stool to the dock and produce my favourite layered style using a spray bottle and scissors.

The most memorable of Michael's cuts was the one he had in Bhutan. We were walking the streets of Paro and saw the universal candy cane sign of a barber shop. Inside the small room were two chairs. In the first a man's face was underneath a mass of foam ready for a shave and the second was empty. Using mime

Michael was able to communicate that he wanted a haircut. The barber quickly placed Michael in the chair and began spraying his hair with water from a plant mister. The barber then pulled out the biggest pair of scissors I have ever seen. These scissors were larger than shears used to cut cloth. With these huge scissors the barber cut Michael's hair like an expert. A head massage and oiling were also part of the price. Michael left feeling relaxed and ready to face the next day of travel.

*****

Teaching at the International School of Dhaka

The International School of Dhaka (ISD) had been started by a group of businessmen in 1999 as a non-profit English medium school. The school followed the International Baccalaureate Curriculum from kindergarten to grade twelve. Graduates were accepted by universities in North America and the UK as well locally. The International School of Dhaka was part of a large business conglomerate which included hospitals and factories. It meant that budget expenditures were closely monitored by internal and external financial departments. Like Moscow, there was no guarantee that what teachers ordered would arrive. Again, Michael and I learned to make do with what we had and did not count on materials arriving in a timely manner.

The science department consisted of specialized science rooms where physics, chemistry, biology, and middle school science classes were taught. Supplies for experiments were kept in a storage room and organized and distributed by two lab technicians. In my first year, the two technicians barely spoke to each other. Both were poorly qualified for the job. Supplies were not cataloged or organized well and there was no guarantee that I would receive the equipment I asked for.

At the beginning of my second year one of the technicians was replaced by a young man with a science degree from the United Kingdom. What a difference. He readily understood my requests for equipment and chemicals. He spoke Bangla as well as English. Using contacts at the local university, he found alternatives for items that were unattainable due to cost or customs regulations. Boxes sitting on the shelves in the supply room were finally opened and many wonderful resources were found and used.

The majority of the students at the International School of Dhaka (ISD) were Bangladeshi nationals. This was very different from Moscow where the student body was multicultural and the common language spoken was English. At ISD the common language was Bangla and English was only spoken to teachers, and the occasional foreign student.

The level of English proficiency in my classes varied significantly. Unlike some of my colleagues, I did not get angry when students spoke their first language in my classes. I knew that learning in a second language was exhausting. Speaking to their friends in their mother tongue helped them understand what to do. I could tell by their actions that most of the conversations in Bangla were related to the assignment they were working on, and these eventually had to be written in English. I became an English Language teacher as well as a science teacher. My students could show their understanding by using diagrams and bullet points. I did not ask them to write grammatically correct sentences when they only had a small amount of English vocabulary to choose from.

Teachers ate lunch at the school cafeteria where most of the meals were Bangladeshi curries, dahl, and rice dishes. Our teaching schedule also had a mid-morning break. At this time two men prepared tea and coffee for us in the teachers' lounge. For special occasions traditional samosas and other deep-fried treats were served along with cake. My waistline grew at a steady rate while in Bangladesh.

******

The International School of Dhaka organized yearly field trips for the students in middle and high school. Designed by the middle year's coordinator and supported by teachers, the aim was to provide students with experiences that promoted global mindedness. I accompanied the grade six students on their three-day boat cruise. The boat motored up and down the main river that ran through Dhaka.

We got off the boat for tours of local biscuit and paper factories. Instructional time was built into the daily schedule. For science we tested water for pH and temperature and collected samples from different areas of the river for comparison. The students drew pictures of scenery for art and they created paper boats for design technology. Interviews with the locals and letter writing were done for English and humanities. Yoga on the foredeck and soccer with the children of the local village rounded out the physical education part of the trip.

Parents feared kidnapping attempts and robbery; therefore, the boat had armed guards and we did not leave the metropolitan area. We motored south the first day and only a few students noticed that we had backtracked on the second day. We passed under the same bridges and passed our starting point to anchor on the northern outskirts of town.

******

As one of the grade ten biology teachers, I accompanied the students to Tioman Island, Indonesia. The school had an annual contract with the educational organization Ecofieldtrips and we stayed at their Melina Beach Resort. Their weeklong programs focused on environmental issues such as logging and global warming, as well as team building.

The ISD Tioman trip combined social studies and biology. For the social studies' task students interviewed locals and asked how tourism had influenced their lives. The Ecofieldtrip guides were graduates of university biology or environmental systems programs and some were working on master's degrees. They loved teaching our group about the environment. Consequently, our students' confidence in analysing data grew. We walked to the rainforest and measured the height and diameter of trees. On the tidal flats we counted the numbers of different species of crabs. Our guides told us how mangrove trees adapted to live in salt water, and the students surveyed the intertidal zones for species diversity. Coral reefs were a short boat ride away and students had the opportunity to snorkel to see tropical fish. Tioman Island was a beautiful reprieve from the big city.

******

Criminal underbelly

In South Korea we befriended a teacher who had worked at the International School of Dhaka. She had left the year before we arrived. Our shared experiences with poverty, beggars, and staring were common topics across the lunch table. During one of these conversations our friend disclosed that her purse had been snatched after a dinner out at the Dutch club.

Dhaka was not a safe place to live if you had money. Thieves were opportunistic and tenacious. The bars on the windows and high walls with barbed wire at the top were helpful deterrents. Armed guards were employed by apartment and strip mall owners. Any business that wanted to keep beggars and thieves out had guards at the entrances to their parking areas and entrances.

Michael and I got used to the presence of the armed guards outside our neighborhood shops and businesses. What we did not truly understand was that hired guards indicated that there was a complete lack of official law enforcement in the city. The Rapid Action Battalion or RAB that we saw driving around our neighborhood were an elite group assigned to fight organized crime, not petty criminals. We were told by local teachers that the RAB were politically controlled and had a reputation of making people "disappear."

To maintain order, it was common practice for guards to cane rickshaw drivers. The rickshaw drivers needed written permission to cross the guard line to our residential areas or to be carrying residents. The Baridhara district rickshaw drivers had to wear pants and not the usual lungi. Watching men being caned was upsetting, but the locals either stopped to watch or kept on walking as if nothing unusual was happening. Being beaten was an accepted immediate punishment for minor infractions.

The opportunistic thieves of Dhaka took things that were easy to snatch. A colleague had a bicycle stolen from his sixth-floor apartment balcony. He checked the bars on the balcony occasionally to make sure they were secure. One day he noticed one was loose. The next night the thieves who had started the process removed the bar completely and stole the bicycle. Our friend was not pleased by the theft of his bicycle, but he was impressed by their courage to climb six floors.

Groups of thieves regularly waited outside embassy clubs in the late evening as it was dark and their targets had had a few drinks. Women climbing onto rickshaws would place their purses on their laps or over their shoulders. They were easily snatched by thieves driving by on motorcycles. Even though this was a common occurrence nothing was done to dissuade the groups of thieves lingering outside the clubs.

Our colleague had her purse snatched just a few blocks from where she lived. Her purse was over her shoulder and the thieves grabbed in as they drove by on a motorcycle. Taking some responsibility for the robbery, since she had not placed her purse in the seat compartment, she was surprised at how quickly it happened and how powerless she was to stop it. The incident affected her both physically and mentally. She required physiotherapy for her injured shoulder and the incident unsettled her to the point that she took a new job in China rather than renew her contract at ISD. Purse snatching remained a problem throughout the time we were there. Everyone was vulnerable.

In January of 2011 we signed contracts for a third year. We had not seen any job vacancies at other international schools that matched our profiles. Living in Bangladesh was difficult, but our teaching colleagues, as well as the students, were great to work with. Plus, we knew that we were making a difference in the learning experiences of the students, which was rewarding.

Once we decided to stay in Dhaka, Michael and I thought that owning or renting a car would decrease our reliance on the van system and give us a little more freedom to do things on weekends. In our search for a car one of the van drivers volunteered to help us. He set up some test drives of cars that were being sold by a friend of his. These cars required immediate repair work and we decided not to buy any of them.

The van driver was not pleased when he heard that we were not going to buy a car from his friend. We were adamant that we did not want any of the used cars that his friend had shown us. Shortly after this conversation Michael and I were victims of a well-orchestrated armed robbery where our personal computers and school bags were stolen. We had our suspicions.

On the morning of the theft, Michael and I stepped out of the gate of our apartment expecting the shuttle van to be coming around the corner within the minute. It was 0630 and they were never late. While we stood there wondering what was keeping the van, a car pulled up and stopped. I thought that they were lost and stopping to ask for directions. In hindsight this thought was extremely naïve! Who would be lost at 0630 in the morning in a residential area of Dhaka?

As I was looking at the car the doors opened and five men leaped out and ran towards us. Two had canes like the ones used to beat rickshaw drivers, one had a sickle with a curved blade that did not look too nice, and the fourth had what looked like a real gun. The fifth quickly grabbed the briefcase full of student work that I had put by my feet. Three of them attacked Michael who was so surprised that he just gave them his computer bag while they struck him with the sticks and threatened him with the sickle. The one with the gun pointed it at me while the man who took my briefcase returned for my computer bag, which I had on my shoulder.

As I looked at the gun I was confident that it was a toy. At which point I decided that I didn't want to give my computer up so easily and held on to the strap. A short tug of war ensued with the one with the toy gun yelling and jumping up and down. The man with the sickle turned towards me and lifted the blade to cut the strap that was between me and the thief. At this point I heard Michael yelling to let go, so I did. The men all jumped back into the car and drove away. In less than a minute our personal computers, school and house keys, and a lot of graded student work was gone.

The school van arrived as the car drove away and we tried to make sense of what had just happened. Shaking and disoriented we were told by the building guards that the incident needed to be reported to the police as soon as possible. Someone had written the license number of the car down. We called the school to tell them we had been robbed and needed to go to the police station. The school's director came to our building as soon as he heard the news and helped organize transport.

After composing ourselves Michael and I were driven to the Gulshan police station. Gulshan was one of the most affluent areas of Dhaka, but when we walked through the doors of the police station there was nothing modern about it. Two older wooden desks with chairs in front of them were located on the right. A battered cloth couch leaned against the wall on the left. Designed and built before central air conditioning the doors and windows were open.

I was told to sit on the couch while Michael went to the desk to fill in a crime report. The floors were dirty and the only technology to be seen was a dial phone and a walkie-talkie system. The bookcases behind the desks were completely full of files with more piled on top reaching to the ceiling. All the files had layers of dust on them. We were sitting in the stereotypical developing world police station. To add to the ambiance the officer sitting in front of Michael spit at least five feet out the door before acknowledging his presence.

Our van driver acted as interpreter and Michael was instructed to write a statement describing what we remembered of the attack. The officer picked up the roll of butcher paper which was on his desk and tore off two equal sized pieces. He then searched his drawer and produced a sheet of carbon paper. I hadn't seen carbon paper in years and this piece was well worn. Michael raised his eyebrows and had to smile as he positioned the carbon paper between the two pieces of paper before writing his statement.

The robbery had happened so quickly we could not remember anything specific about the thieves other than they had worn western clothing and not lungis. The car had been white with blackened windows, but most cars in Dhaka were white with blacked windows. When checked, the license plate had been stolen from a car in Sylhet in the northern part of Bangladesh. There was no immediate way of tracking the car or the thieves. After our visit to the police station Michael and I realized that there was little hope of getting our computers back.

The thieves had watched our travel routines and planned meticulously. Our computer bags were only available for snatching during the one-to-two-minute window at 0630 in the morning when we stepped outside the gate of our building to get into the van. At school Michael and I got in and out of the van within the guarded school grounds. When we returned home at the end of the day we got out of the van and walked straight into the underground parking lot. Whoever planned the theft organized the blockage of the van for the two to three minutes that they needed to steal our belongings.

The police reassured us that they were trying to find the assailants. Two of them came to the school a week later to give an update, which was no news. They were very apologetic and assured us that they were doing everything possible. About a month later they asked us to come in to see if we could identify a suspect they had caught. We were taken to the back of the police station to another office with stacked files on bookcases and decrepit furniture similar to the front office. We were asked to sit down and once settled they brought out a man who was barefoot and only wearing a lungi. His hands and ankles were shackled and he was in a sorry condition. We reiterated that the men who attacked us had worn western clothes, pants, and shirts as well as shoes, plus they had been driving a car which meant they were organized and not a petty thief like this man obviously was.

Michael was surprised and annoyed that the school did not help us replace our stolen computers. Our personal computers were needed to deliver content to classes. Antiquated classroom computers did not have the software to run a power point presentation. Our computers had to be replaced as soon as possible, so we bought new computers at full retail cost while recovering from the stress of being assaulted.

Michael developed bruises on his arms where the thieves had struck him with the canes. I had grazes from the strap as it was pulled from my arm, but neither of us had been cut. The most unnerving thing about the experience was the realization that there was no operational police system in Dhaka. Law enforcement was a charade. Property was protected by walls and privately paid guards who were subject to bribery.

******

Though physically fine, Michael and I were both mentally traumatized by the incident. Unfortunately, the school had no formal mechanism to help us deal with the stress we were experiencing. The school counsellors expertise was childhood anxiety, learning disorders, and abuse, not post-traumatic stress disorder. We did not feel safe and had the door locks changed immediately. We also insisted that the school move us to a recently vacated apartment in Baridhara, a more secure neighbourhood.

Even though our new apartment was in the safer diplomatic neighbourhood it did not alleviate my fear of going out. My distrust of strangers and imagined attacks did not abate. I never felt safe and lived in a high stress fight-or-flight mode, typical of post-traumatic stress disorder. Seeing white cars with blackened windows brought back the terror of the armed robbery. These cars were everywhere. I was continually reliving the incident during the day and at night in my dreams.

The local newspaper, *The Daily Ittefak*, published a report on February 21st, 2011 and a copy was given to me by a staff member of the school. Google translated the piece from Bangla as;

"Canadian Couple Mugged and dragged by bleaded instrument in Gulshan." Google translated the title as "Canadian Couple Stripped of Gold." "A Canadian couple Michael Gao and his wife Kate Rain (Kate Binns) was going to ISD by Rickshaw. When they arrived at the road 126 of Gulshan 2, a private car consisting of 4 muggers blocked their way. Then the muggers dragged the couple by bleaded instrument and took gold ornaments, mobile sets and asset of 2 lakh taka from the couple."

I am not sure what the proper translation for "bleaded" instruments was and we did not have physical "gold", but metaphorically our work computers and documents were "gold" to us. Some of the objects taken in my school bags that day were irreplaceable.

It took years of living in countries with effective police and social systems before I stopped having flashbacks of the assault and theft of our computer bags. In Thailand and South Korea

I was not worried about my personal safety and my trust in the goodness of others slowly returned.

******

Bhutan

Shortly after the armed robbery, Michael and I flew to the Buddhist Kingdom of Bhutan with four teaching friends. The weeklong holiday had been booked through a Bhutan government agency — all foreigner tourists were required to be accompanied by an official guide. There were various tours offered, including kayaking and hiking tours. We decided on the cultural tour that showed us the most countryside.

My immediate impression of Bhutan was that it was quiet, clean, and friendly. With a total population of 700,000 most of the citizens lived in houses or three to four story apartment buildings. Not densely populated Bhutan was the complete opposite of the noisy and dirty city of Dhaka.

Bhutan's Government organizational chart included a Ministry of Happiness under which all other government divisions fit. The Bhutanese believed that being happy in what you did was the most important thing in life. When the government census was done, one of the things they calculated was the Gross National Happiness of the population. In 2015 over 80% of the population stated they were either extremely happy or moderately happy and less than 10% stated they were unhappy. These were incredible statistics for a country that did not have a large GDP and most of the population were farmers who lived outside of the main city of Thimpu.

The Bhutanese were committed to maintaining their cultural traditions. The country did not permit large scale tourism in order to prevent the exploitation and ecological harm that occurred in Nepal. Small tour groups were government run and tourist numbers closely monitored. The cost of going to Bhutan started at $200.00 a day and a variety of tours were available.

When we visited in 2011, televisions were a recent addition to houses and the Internet had just become available. The capital city of Thimpu had no traffic lights. The busiest intersection had a box in the center with a traffic warden directing traffic. When the idea of a traffic light was brought up the governing body of the city voted it down.

In Thimpu wearing national dress was encouraged and citizens usually wore the cultural clothing of their ancestors. Our guide told us that if you worked for the government it was mandatory to wear the national dress. The preservation of their culture was a top priority.

The international airport was located in Paro, a short drive away from Thimpu. Flying into Paro on Dragon Air was an experience. The city itself, nestled in the Himalaya Mountain range, was over two kilometres above sea level and a challenge to fly into. Airplanes had to fly very close to the sides of the mountains as they approached the runway. Only Druk Air and Dragon Airline pilots had been trained to land at the airport, and there were no other international flights. The airport was small and only a few passenger flights arrived and departed each day.

Michael and I arrived with our golf clubs as we were going to Nepal to play in Kathmandu for the last part of the holiday. Surprised to see the clubs, our tour guide told us that there was a nine-hole golf course in Thimpu. Officially the highest golf course in the world, the course was used by businessmen, diplomats, and members of the Bhutanese royal family. We told our guide that we would love to play. He talked to his superiors and arranged a time for us to play when we returned from our cultural tour.

We stayed in Thimpu for a few days to acclimatize to the higher elevation. During this time we visited local temples and a large Buddha statue that overlooked the city. On the way down from the statue we stopped at an animal enclosure that housed Takin, the national animal of Bhutan. Takin were strange looking. A cross between a goat and an antelope, they are only found in Bhutan.

Our group stopped at a traditional market selling fruits and vegetables as well as clothing. It was located in front of an old fortress that had been converted into government offices. The traditional Bhutanese clothing was very attractive, and Michael and I both bought coats and skirts to take back to Dhaka with us.

Our cultural tour of Bhutan included driving in a comfortable van to the historic Dzongs, or fortress-monasteries, located around the country. The complexes had tall white walls with high ornate wooden windows on the outside. Inside the buildings were beautifully painted with murals of Buddha's journey to enlightenment. Full of monks of all ages, the Dzongs provided peaceful educational and spiritual retreats to the population of Bhutan.

Driving over the high mountain passes was a bit frightening. The roads were narrow and there were no safety barriers to stop vehicles from going over the edge. Michael found it humorous to call our attention to the steep drops as we were driving by the more dramatic chasms. When not worrying about our lives we saw Langur monkeys and appreciated the huge forests of rhododendrons. These flowering trees had been imported to the Canadian west coast and I had smaller versions in my garden.

As we drove through villages and small towns it was common to see pictures of phalluses on the walls of houses and buildings. Our guide told us that the drawings were inspired by an ancient folk tale. The paintings were intended to drive away the evil eye and malicious gossip. The Dzongs and temples did not display the phallus, but most of the rural houses had at least one colorful penis drawn on them.

The furthest we went in Bhutan was to the Phobjikha valley, a bird sanctuary dedicated to the black necked crane. The crane was an endangered species that formed lifelong breeding pairs. The birds migrated to the Tibetan Plateau to breed, but spend the winters in Bhutan. When we were there most of the birds had already flown north, but we saw a lone male whose mate had died. Single birds did not migrate and we were lucky to see such a rare bird.

The last day of our cultural tour was spent climbing to the famous Tiger's Nest or Paro Taktsang Monastery. The monastery was built on the cliff side three thousand metres above sea level and only accessible by walking up a trail. I could barely see the buildings from the valley floor. We could rent donkeys to carry us halfway up. But, as we were relatively fit, we all declined the offer.

We started out in good spirits mentally prepared for the challenge of hiking up a steep mountain trail. Our guide was a bit concerned that we would not make it to the monastery before it closed. He knew how long tourists took to climb the distance and we were starting out later than he would have liked.

The climb was steep and relentless, but luckily resting places were frequent. After a few hours of walking, we had made it to the halfway point. There was a cafe built there, so we stopped for a short break and used the toilets. A member of our group had bad knees and he decided to stay at the café and rejoin us on the descent.

The rest of us continued to the top, taking more and more breaks as the air got thinner and thinner. We reached the monastery perched on the cliff edge with enough time to enjoy the peaceful setting. After lighting a candle, we took a brief tour of the monastery before descending. Going down was easier on the lungs, but it was still a workout for my prairie girl legs.

On our final day in Thimpu we waved goodbye to the others as they headed to the Indian border by bus. Michael, the guide, and I went to the golf course. On our arrival we learned that a member of the royal family was on the course. This meant that the stricter dress code of no bare legs for men or women was being enforced. Luckily, we had the correct clothing in our bags and we quickly changed.

Our tour guide was keen to try to hit a ball and we suggested he try a seven iron. Even wearing his traditional coat, which was bulky, he managed to hit the ball down the fairway and, in some instances, he managed to hit the ball farther than either Michael or me. This made us all laugh and we encouraged him to continue to play in the future.

Bhutan was a beautiful place and we hoped to return one day.

******

Time to move on

On our return to Dhaka from Bhutan the full intensity of the city struck me. After living there for two years I concluded that the social and cultural systems were not changing any time soon. Large scale foreign aid donations had not improved the lives of the millions who lived there, partly due to corruption and nepotism.

In addition to being the victim of crime I had been treated poorly by the administration team when I applied for leadership roles. Though I was fully qualified with years of experience in leadership the new principal's wife was awarded the coordinator role. My understanding at my interview for head of department was that they would award the role internally. When I saw the role listed in the external databases attached to the chemistry vacancy, I withdrew my application. The head of department role was being used to attract candidates to the vacancy. My desire to do the job was secondary.

Michael and I decided that we needed to move to a country with a better police system and a school that valued my expertise. It was late in the hiring season and there were no direct matches for our qualifications in the databanks. Positions existed in the Middle East, but we worried about the political unrest in the region. With no job opportunities Michael phoned shipping companies and researched the process of repatriating to Canada.

As we were preparing to return to Canada, we received an email from the principal who had hired us in Bangkok. He had taken a position as the director of the American Pacific School in Chiangmai. He offered Michael a position as a computer teacher with additional responsibilities running and maintaining the IT systems infrastructure. A middle/high school science vacancy was available for me. We were interested as living at a school located outside of Chiangmai would be quieter and less stressful than living in Dhaka.

In subsequent conversations we noted that the salary package was half of what we were being paid in Dhaka and the school provided flights home every two years, not annually. Teacher apartments were located on campus and the job description included boarding house responsibilities once a week. On the other hand, we would be able to transport our eight cubic meters of personal belongings using the International School of Dhaka's shipment allowance and the Thai school's shipping connections.

After considering the offer for a week we accepted. The decision to take a job in Thailand was easy to make based on our financial reality. The director made our new jobs sound like we were going to be instrumental in making the American Pacific International School a better place for students. We embraced the challenge of building a curriculum to make learning more interactive and memorable.

Chapter 3:
Thailand 2011-2013

"we arrived with all our luggage, it is really nice to be in a developed world...our first stop was a new mall that had EVERYTHING you could possibly think of...amazing"

(Facebook Aug 2011)

Starting from the moment we landed at the small airport in Chiangmai, my two years in Thailand was a restorative experience. My stress symptoms decreased and my trust in others was restored. In stark contrast to the Dhaka airport, the atmosphere at the Chiangmai airport was friendly and welcoming.

The airport was full of foreigners either arriving for their vacation or leaving for their next destination and it was refreshing to see the diversity of people walking around. I was frequently the only white woman on planes in and out of Bangladesh. If I happened to spot another white woman she was usually attached to a foreign business, NGO or employed by our school or the American school. In Thailand we saw equal numbers of men and women in all types of western dress from high-end fashion to low-end budget deals. Western clothes revealed more skin than would have been allowed in Dhaka and it was a bit shocking at first.

Chiangmai airport was not large, basically a two-story building with the domestic terminal on one end and the international terminal on the other. The two luggage conveyor belts were busy places with the continuous arrival of both domestic and international flights. Taxi drivers tried to entice arriving passengers into their cars as they had in Moscow. At a taxi booth located in the terminal fares were posted and guaranteed.

Chiangmai had a population of approximately two hundred thousand and was in the northern part of Thailand. The historic old city centre was square and surrounded by stone walls and a moat. Designated a UNESCO world heritage site there were many temples and museums to visit. Michael and I easily walked around the moat in an hour if we didn't stop along the way to look at the shops and temples. Large shade trees along the moat provided a cool respite during the hot summer months.

We enjoyed going to the weekly Sunday Market, which attracted more local artisans than the Night Market. The main centre streets as well as some side streets were closed to traffic, so tourists and locals did not have to worry about being run over. One of the attractions of the main street was the variety of food vendors and eating-places within the temples that lined it. Mango sticky rice, pad Thai, and fried gyoza were our favourite choices.

The Sunday market ran from four o'clock to midnight. At six o'clock the locals would stand and sing the national anthem. The accompanying music was played over the public speaker system. The King of Thailand had written the anthem. The music was even played inside public places, like movie theatres, before the shows started.

The markets added to the charm of living in Thailand. There were numerous places to take our friends and relatives when they came to visit. We shopped, golfed, took cooking lessons and signed up for day tours to elephant sanctuaries and temples. Later, we discovered Chiangrai and the northern tracts where the hill tribes lived.

Our new school was located about forty minutes southwest of the southern city limit on the Hangdong and Samoeng road. At a higher elevation than the city it was cooler, a benefit especially during the hottest months of the year. The road to the school campus was narrow and winding. Chickens and dogs would run out unexpectedly or traffic would stop suddenly when drivers decided to buy some fruit from the stalls at the sides of the roads. The mix of cars, motorcycles and the residents' activities along the road always made the drive up and down this road exciting. Driving in Thailand required defensive skills — we learned to expect the unexpected at any given time regardless of where we were.

******

Living on campus

Our new home was on the third floor of an apartment building within the school campus. The three-story building was located at the end of a short street perpendicular to the administration block. There was no elevator. Michael and I had to carry our luggage, weekly groceries, and anything else we purchased up three flights of stairs.

Our apartment had a spacious open concept living room and kitchen. Doors on the left led to two large bedrooms, both with ensuite bathrooms. In the kitchen there was a fridge and a gas stove with the cylinder of natural gas in the cupboard beside it. The water came from a reservoir up the hill, and was not treated. We could not drink it, so we purchased twenty-litre jugs of potable water on a routine basis for a minimal amount.

The water coming from the kitchen sink taps was the same temperature as the outside reservoir, but the lack of hot water in the kitchen was not usually an issue. We ate stir-fries and one-pot meals cooked in our wok, so cleanup was quick and easy with lukewarm water. If we needed hot water, we boiled water in our kettle and added it to the dishwater in the sink. Small 10-litre water heaters in the bathrooms provided hot water for showers and hand washing.

Another peculiar thing in the kitchen was the oven. It didn't have a bottom panel. When I opened the door to see how large it was, I looked directly down at the floor. Consequently, we did not bake anything in there and bought a small toaster oven from Tesco's for our baking needs.

Temperatures climbed to over 30°Celsius in Thailand. The windows had only one pane of glass and had visible gaps around the frames. Hot air from outside entered easily. We had one air conditioning unit for the whole apartment, located in the main bedroom. The unit did not cool the main living areas, so Michael set up fans to help spread the cool air around the apartment.

Starting in February, we used the conditioner full time when we were in the house. We put our mattress on the floor where the coolest air was, which allowed us to sleep at the hottest time of the year, the month of April. One day the air conditioning unit stopped working. The repairman said something that we still remember to this day. He told us that if we had not used the air conditioning unit so much it would not have broken, an example of the Thai approach to problems. Theoretically this is very true, but realistically we needed the air conditioning unit to cool the place to a reasonable 26° Celsius from the outside temperature of 36° Celsius. Michael and I repeat these words of wisdom whenever something electrical stops working, "if we had not used it, it would not have broken."

******

Ban Tawai- furniture, paper and pottery

Our apartment in Thailand was sparsely furnished compared to the Moscow and Dhaka apartments. One queen-sized bed, an uncomfortable wicker loveseat, two heavy wooden tables with two wooden chairs, and a kitchen starter kit that we were told had to be returned as soon as possible. Our shipment from Dhaka did not include furniture; we had downsized from twelve cubic meters to eight cubic meters. When we asked about the lack of furniture the director informed us that the Thai owner assumed that we would buy what we needed. Furniture in Thailand was cheap.

To buy teak and other wooden furniture, we drove a short distance to Ban Tawai, a town and shopping area that specialized in wooden furniture and other hand-crafted products. Michael and I went there frequently. We bought wooden carvings as well as custom furniture. We filled our apartment with two teak couches, two armchairs, a coffee table, and side tables for our bed. We also purchased three Thai style cabinets to use as bookcases.

Along the eastern side of Chiangmai were more wooden carving shops as well as places to buy traditional Thai silk, pottery, and paper products. Michael and I bought a complete dinner set of Thai pottery to be shipped back to Canada as well as decorative pillow covers for our living room. Paper umbrella shops and other places that sold mulberry paper products were a main source of presents for our families. When we left Thailand, we shipped home a twenty cubic metre container filled with beautiful Thai furniture and carvings in addition to our possessions gathered in Moscow and Bangladesh.

******

Elephants

The Elephant Nature Park was started by Lek Chailert to provide sanctuary to rescued elephants. The elephants came from the tourist and logging industries as well as the streets of Bangkok. The non-profit organization saved the elephants from being euthanized.

Friends of ours volunteered at the Elephant Nature Park over the years and helped prepare food for the elephants and other animals that lived there. The sanctuary was magical, with elephants roaming freely. Their mahouts or keepers did not interfere with their movements unless necessary for safety.

Lek Chailert was a caring soul who had a special attachment to elephants. Michael and I went to the Nature Park twice and were fortunate enough to meet her on one of these trips. She was preparing to be interviewed by a journalist, but she had some time to talk to us. She asked if we wanted to see an elephant that was very sick and dying. A once in a lifetime opportunity, we agreed and walked with her to an area that was off limits to regular tour groups.

An elderly elephant was lying on its side against a man-made mound of dirt. The "pillow" helped her breathe more easily. The vet was overseeing an intravenous drip hanging on a pole that was providing fluids and pain medications. The goal was to keep the elephant comfortable. It was a special opportunity to be that close to such a noble animal being looked after by people who cared.

The elephants that lived in the park had a daily feeding and washing routine. When we visited, we fed the elephants from a building that was elevated off the ground. We were also invited to wash some of the elephants in the river. Lectures and hand-outs gave us information about the plight of the Asian elephants. A delicious vegetarian lunch was included in the entrance fee.

******

Massages

As an athlete I used massage therapy and saunas to treat muscle injuries. When we moved to Moscow, Michael and I heard about a masseuse from our colleagues. Our badminton training sessions with Marina caused all kinds of muscle pain, so we asked Olga if she would add us to her list of regulars. She agreed and came to our apartment on a weekly basis to give us deep tissue Swedish oil massages.

Bangladesh did not offer massage services other than those in the spas of the Radisson and Westin hotels, so when we arrived in Thailand we were happy that massages were easily available. Just down the street from our apartment was a garage-like building that offered Thai massages for the equivalent of three US dollars an hour. There were four mattresses on the floor and the front was completely open to the road. Everyone wore loose fitting Thai pants and shirts when being massaged so no skin was exposed. The masseuse's qualifications were framed and hung on the wall. Their regular client list included locals and many of the teachers from the school. In our first year Michael and I walked down there on a regular basis to get "fine-tuned."

During my second year at the American Pacific International School I re-injured my lower back when moving a heavy chair. The pain was terrible and I could not stand or sit for more than a few minutes. I called in sick and stayed at home taking pain killers and doing back exercises. When our house cleaner saw how badly I was doing she phoned her friend who was a masseuse. Her friend agreed to come to our apartment and give me a massage treatment.

The qualified masseuse had an innate sense of where to press and stretch to achieve the desired results and my reluctant muscles slowly started to relax. The daily treatment enabled me to go back to work within a week. I asked the masseuse if she would continue to come to my apartment to give me massages to improve my range of motion. She agreed.

On one of her visits Michael asked if he could have massages as well. The next time she brought a friend, and it was the beginning of a routine where Michael and I had Thai massages three times a week in our apartment. I lay on the bed while Michael set up a padded area in the living room. Their fee was a little more than the group along the road at $5.00/hour. The massages cured my back pain and gave me physical and mental health relief for the remainder of the year.

******

Teaching at APIS

My science room at the American Pacific International School (APIS) was in the basement of the building that held the cafeteria and the library. For various reasons the teaching materials and consumables were not organized when I arrived. They were piled in two storage rooms. Much of my first year at APIS was spent checking and discarding equipment that did not work. This included a very expensive spectrometer which had been placed on a back shelf for years and had rusted in the humid air.

I repurposed a shelving unit and sorted through boxes of materials that had been left unopened. As in Moscow and Bangladesh, the equipment and replacement consumables were ordered by the outgoing teacher to suit what they were planning to do before they left. When the boxes arrived the following school year the new teacher would not necessarily want the materials or even know what was in the boxes if they did not take the initiative to open them. Opening the boxes unearthed all kinds of great things that my teaching partner and I used in our lessons.

Of more concern to me was the chemical storage room which was a complete mess. The odour of volatile carbon compounds was distinctive and hazardous. Liquids had been left in unlabeled glass beakers and the sink area was not clean. When I looked at the shelves the chemicals were placed alphabetically, and some labels were illegible. There were no cabinets for acids or flammable chemicals. All the chemicals were stored on the open shelves. I found a total of twenty-eight litres of sulphuric acid in various sizes of bottles. It was unlikely that the high school chemistry classes would use more than a litre a year.

For peace of mind, I reorganized the chemicals according to the Philip Harris recommended storage system and advocated for a proper ventilation system. My request resulted in two ten-inch fans being placed into the windows venting into a hallway that was open to the outside. The solution was not the best choice, but it was better than nothing.

******

Proper chemical storage was a recurring problem in the international schools where I worked. In Moscow, the high school chemical storage room was overcrowded. The potential for accidents and spillage was high. Surprisingly for a new school, proper storage cabinets were not provided for the flammable liquids and acids. I advocated for proper safety equipment with the safety officer. The result was that a second room was designated for the storage of the physics equipment and proper chemical cabinets were ordered. An extraction fan was installed in a window to improve air quality and the technician was very thankful.

At the Anglo-American School I found chemicals in the middle school classrooms which had not been returned to the main chemical storage room. These chemicals included a bottle of solid sodium. A highly reactive soft metal, sodium was used to demonstrate exothermic reactions. A small piece of sodium would react with water to create sodium hydroxide and hydrogen. Once started it would burn until all the sodium was gone. If too much sodium was put into water the reaction was explosive.

A middle school teacher in Moscow decided to demonstrate the power of the sodium-water reaction to his grade eight class. Placing a bucket of water in the middle of the courtyard he positioned the students at a distance that he considered safe. He then threw a large piece of sodium into the water and ran back to the safety of the group. The sodium reacted with the water immediately with a loud explosive bang as well as a large cloud of white smoke. The bucket was in pieces and the windows of all the classrooms surrounding the courtyard shook.

When teachers and administrators heard the explosion and saw the smoke, they thought the worst. The event caused undue stress to many staff and students. The teacher was reprimanded and left at the end of the year. When I asked the students what they had learned from the demonstration they could not tell me anything more than that there had been an explosion. The demonstration had not helped them learn or remember anything specific about chemical reactions.

Years later, a colleague had a similar mishap during a demonstration. She had practiced earlier using the correct safety equipment to ensure the safety of students, including a thick plastic barrier wall. When the piece of sodium was placed on the water it caught fire as predicted, but it moved to the side of the glass container and got stuck on the glass. The direct heat of the reaction caused the glass container to break with an explosive shattering noise. The gases and heat from the reaction set off the fire alarm causing the immediate evacuation of the school.

No one was hurt that day, but from a safety perspective, I did not understand why this dangerous demonstration continued to be supported by chemistry teachers. There was a plethora of chemicals, including baking soda and vinegar, which could be used to demonstrate chemical reactions. The chances of any student seeing or using pure sodium in real life were miniscule since it was only used in nuclear power plants.

*****

I had many positive experiences when teaching at the American Pacific International School (APIS). Thai culture valued teachers, and parents believed a good education improved future opportunities for their children. At the beginning of the year there was a ceremony where the students thanked their teachers and gave us flowers. At the end of the year there was a ceremony where teachers gave students words of wisdom and good wishes for the following year.

******

APIS was a boarding school so lunch was provided to staff and students. The food was generally good. Our students would warn us away from the more traditional dishes like boiled chicken feet and pig blood soup. Many of the dishes were "Thai" spicy. We got accustomed to the burning tongue and instant sweat from the chili pastes, and began to appreciate the uniqueness of Thai cuisine.

I traveled with the grade eleven and twelves to an outdoor education facility in the Maekong valley located in the northern part of Thailand. The owners were retired teachers who, like Ecofieldtrips, had designed the facility to house large school groups. Programs included outdoor education treks suitable for the Duke of Edinburgh Award, Community Service projects that linked directly into the IB diploma Core commitments, as well as Team building games and cooking activities.

Our trip combined team building and community service activities for the students. The first year we helped repair a school building and in the second our students taught primary school children some simple English vocabulary words in the morning. In the afternoons the students participated in team activities which culminated with building a raft and floating down the river.

Public school classrooms in Thailand, Nepal, and Bhutan demonstrated how class size affected the activities students could engage in. In all three countries these classrooms were full of desks and students with barely enough room to walk between the rows. Lecturing at the front of the class was the most efficient way to teach large numbers of students, while inquiry-based activities would have been limited. I appreciated the smaller class sizes of international schools where the teacher could be a mentor guiding student learning and where students had space to work in groups independently.

******

Gender identity

Thailand was a very welcoming and tolerant country when it came to sexual orientation. In general, the citizens of Thailand did not have strict male and female roles or expectations of dress. It was not unusual to be served by an androgynous male or female. Clothing and demeanour could not be relied on to identify specific gender identities.

Transgender "lady boys" were easier to identify as they were more flamboyant. Within the culture there was no shame to being gay or lesbian, heterosexual or homosexual, or just plain androgynous. Buddhism was the dominant religion and LGBTQ people were accepted as a "third sex" who were born with these gender identities because of factors from previous incarnations.

A transgender male student enrolled at APIS. He came to school in the boys' uniform and played on the boys' sports teams. At home he dressed as a female and had started the transition process. When the class went for the annual field trip, he appeared at the collection point as a female with hair extensions and women's clothing packed in his bag. In his mind the trip was not "within the school walls" and everyone else on the trip was wearing what they would normally be wearing at home. We couldn't really argue with his logic. We had already arranged a private room for him to sleep in rather than the normal bunking arrangement, so it did not matter if he was male or female on the trip.

******

Social lives restaurants

Phuket, January 1, 2014....life as a expat...today the only thing available on the 10 choice "steak and sea food grill" menu was a pork chop, no steak and no sea food... it appears the vast majority of the choices on the menu were eaten during the new year's feast and have yet to be restocked

- Facebook entry-

While living in Chiangmai Michael and I mainly socialized with our teaching friends. We met in town for dinner before going to Rimping or Tesco's for groceries. A weekly trip down the mountain was necessary to stock up on the food items we needed for the coming week. Rimping, a Thai based supermarket chain, had virtually everything an expat could want. Classical music played in the background as we shopped. The fruits and vegetables were fresh and the meat department provided beef, chicken, and pork. The inventory of dry goods was obviously ordered with the expat population of Chiangmai in mind. Marmite on the shelves indicated that there was a large British population living in the city. A European section also provided yeast and other baking ingredients needed to make cookies and cakes. An instore bakery provided good quality bread while the alcohol section was large with a selection of single malt scotch and imported wine. A minor inconvenience was that stores were not allowed to sell alcohol between 2 pm and 5 pm.

There was a remarkable Thai restaurant a ten-minute walk from our apartment. We called it 'Hill Top' as we had to walk up a very steep driveway. The tables were on a deck that overlooked the hills and mountains. The menu was simple. Our favourites were homemade pad Thai, cashew chicken, green curry, and deep fried dried pork pieces. Dishes were all cooked in a wok, single or double servings. Every dish was made to order and as fresh as fresh could be.

Before we left Thailand, we asked the owners to show us how to cook our favourite meals, which they were happy to do. On our trip to Chiangmai in 2018 Michael and I managed to travel to Hill Top to enjoy the food again. The restaurant had become very popular with the locals after a few well-placed articles in tourist magazines had increased its visibility. Due to their success the owners moved to a larger venue about a hundred meters further up the hill. The new location had an even better view than the first.

For sushi we enjoyed a place called "Sumo Sushi" located in the touristy Nimmanhaemin area. The owner had invented some very tasty fusion roll combinations. Michael enjoyed the seared salmon. My favourites were the dragon and caterpillar rolls. Unfortunately, in 2018 Sumo Sushi was no more, replaced with another business altogether. Michael and I stood outside the door and felt a great loss. We had such good memories of eating there.

The best crème brûlée I have ever eaten was made at Pern's restaurant in Chiangmai. The owner was an accomplished chef from England who had opened the restaurant with the mandatory Thai investor. Pern's was small, but the entrées were excellent. We often went there for the lamb shanks and the crème brûlée. The owner told us the secret to his crème brûlée was the vanilla that he imported specifically for the dessert.

******

Golfing in Thailand

Michael had started playing golf in Dhaka and wanted to continue while working in Thailand. After comparing the various options, we purchased a package at the Mae Jo Golf course. The package included discount rates on the course as well as at their adjoining hotel. We had access to a pool, restaurant, and Thai massages. The downside was that Mae Jo was an hour's drive from our apartment. We would drive there on the weekend, play golf, spend the night, and play again the next day. When friends came, we would book rooms for a few days in order to enjoy the pool and spa facilities, as well as go into Chiangmai. When the days were longer it was possible to play and return the same day.

The Mae Jo golf course was challenging with some particularly memorable holes that only golfers would appreciate. Our friend Tyler called one par 3 the "lava hole." The pit was for water management during the rainy season, but it added to the visual spectacle of the hole. The tee was elevated and we had to hit over the red clay pit to get to the green. Two other holes had large ponds that needed to be crossed—we lost a lot of balls in them. Holes on the back nine had been built to include the original orchards. Once you hit into the trees it was very difficult to get out of them. Many times Michael hit down the row of trees just to pop out the other side rather than try to clear the trees to get back on the fairway.

Closer to home, there was a local nine-hole course at the bottom of the hill. It was only six US dollars a round, but there were no tee times, and it could be very crowded. Visiting Korean players did not have a problem playing with six players rather than the usual four and it slowed play down considerably.

Playing this course could be dangerous—we saw deadly snakes as well as land crabs and fire ants. Some of the greens were like turtle backs and putting a ball into the cup was a challenge. A disco loving person lived next to the course, so it was necessary to tolerate the loud disco beat when playing that hole. The signature hole was an easy seven iron in distance, but challenging to hit since it was surrounded by water. The island hole was the reason we returned to play the nine-hole course. It was so satisfying to land on the green on our first try.

Regardless of the course we played in Thailand, caddies were assigned to us. They would either pull the golf trolley with our clubs or drive the electric golf cart. Caddies were always female and I speculated that this was a labor law to increase the number of jobs for women. As we played, the caddies gave us the distances to the green and were very knowledgeable about which way the ball would travel. They were worth the fee. Michael found out later that caddies would bet on the success of their players. They were truly sorry if their predictions were inaccurate. At Mae Jo,

Michael and I had our favourite caddies who we would ask for specifically when we booked our tee times.

*****

Moving on — philosophical and financial motivation

Our decision to leave Chiangmai at the end of the 2012- 2013 school year was determined by philosophical differences in the delivery of education as well as financial concerns. The budgeting choices of for-profit educational institutions are different from non-profit organizations. The director of the school had been tasked with increasing enrollment to make the school viable financially. To achieve this goal, teachers created a curriculum for all grade levels that was recognized by an outside governing body. Accreditation by external educational organizations was the backbone of a good educational institution and international schools used a variety of organizations to attain this. The principal led the teaching staff in documenting units and completing the necessary forms for accreditation with an Australian governing body called ACS WASC.

News of the change in rigor as well as an active recruitment plan was successful. Enrolment in the middle and high school doubled. I assumed that the increased revenue would be spent on much needed educational materials like desks and teaching consumables needed for the new curriculum. Instead, the owners did not re-invest in resources and the profit went elsewhere. If anything, the situation worsened when profits increased. Ordering resources to teach my overflowing classes became a battle. An eighteen-dollar request for six glue guns to top up my class set was initially denied. I had to reapply with further information to warrant this 'outrageous' expense before the purchase was approved.

The difficulty buying essential educational resources at APIS was hard to tolerate while the school's increased enrolment generated enough income to build a new house on campus beside the classroom block. The school's director was not told what the building was going to be, and we came up with all kinds of theories. We were told later that the owner's daughter moved into the house. Her role at the school was never clarified.

Living in Thailand was wonderful, but our yearly salaries were not substantial. We had taken significant decreases in pay when we signed our contracts and the cost of living in Thailand was increasing. When we asked for a nominal increase in salary after two years, it was denied. We then heard rumours that the owners actually wanted to decrease teachers' salaries. In their opinion the teachers at the school were being paid too much; maintaining good programs did not include expensive experienced teachers. Put together, the lack of salary and poor investment in the school's budget were enough for us to start looking for new job opportunities.

From October to March, we used Search Associates to look for jobs. None fit our criteria of reasonable wages within a non-profit school. Michael had a few email exchanges with two schools in southern Thailand, but neither had science positions. We briefly toyed with the idea of applying for postings in Kazakhstan, but the salary package was not any better than Thailand and we did not fancy going back to cold snowy winters.

Our only option was to return to Canada and find work in the education sector in British Columbia. Repatriation was not straight forward. Michael arranged for a twenty-foot container to ship our personal possessions to Nanaimo, British Columbia. Immigration paperwork and the movement of money and possessions had to be done in the correct sequence to avoid unnecessary taxes. The shipment had to arrive in Canada after us. It took extensive communication with the shippers to arrange the arrival date for a month after we landed in Vancouver. After our final pay cheque, we transferred our money to Canada and closed our accounts. We flew back to Canada via Europe stopping in Copenhagen to see the historical sights and museums before visiting our friend Emily who lived in Amsterdam.

Chapter 4:
Six months in Canada

Amsterdam (De Kas)

Michael and I enjoyed exceptional meals on many occasions while living overseas, prepared by top level chefs. Emily loved good food. When she heard we were coming to the Netherlands she made reservations for us and two other friends at the "chef's table" at the De Kas restaurant. Emily had heard good reviews of the restaurant, and she wanted to give the "chef's table" a try. I had visions of sitting at a table in the main restaurant with the chef visiting for a short time to tell us about his food choices and his life story before heading off back to the kitchen. This is not what we experienced at De Kas.

The restaurant was in a renovated 1926 greenhouse with eight-meter-high glass walls as well as glass ceilings. Located in Frankendael Park, Amsterdam, the view from the windows was spectacular. The owner, Michelin star chef Gert Jan Hageman, wanted to prove that fine dining could have a low carbon foot-print and be sustainable. Menus were seasonal and based on the daily vegetables. Herbs were grown on-site or at farms close by. Meat and fish were also sourced locally. Eating at the chef's table cost 130 Euros per person and included the high-quality wines paired with each course. It was an opportunity that we could not refuse. Emily was moving to her new job in Bangkok, Thailand in the fall.

We arrived at the restaurant at the designated time and were seated at a table on the outside deck. Our first wine appeared with the appetizer and a man dressed like a chef appeared. He was not Gert Jan Hageman, but the newest head chef for this restaurant. He told us that we were his first "chef's table" guests. We accompanied him while he picked edible flowers from the garden beside the deck. As he picked them and put them in a basket, he described the flavours of the flowers.

After collecting the flowers we went into the main kitchen. I had assumed that we would have a table in the main dining room, but was mistaken. Our spot for the evening was a very small table in the corner of the busy kitchen. The table and bench seats were designed for tall people and my feet barely touched the floor.

Our first course was the flowers artistically placed on a plate with a slight sprinkle of dressing—beautiful but not very substantial. The second wine was poured at this stage accompanied by wonderful bread which held off our hunger pains. I could see through the door that the main dining room was full of hungry patrons and the kitchen was in full swing. There were five sous-chefs at specific stations either cooking the steak or salmon or adding the vegetable side dishes. The last station was the dessert station. Watching the chefs get all the meals out at the same time was incredible. The process was finely honed. The head chef gave the final approval on all the plates before they left the kitchen.

At our table we were given information and stories about the history of each dish as they appeared in front of us. Details about the food's origin and the method of cooking were given by the head chef. Everything we tasted was a combination of amazing flavours combined with striking colour and presentation. A new wine glass appeared with each course and each wine complemented the food.

The guests in the main restaurant were served first and we got our plates at the end of each course. Because of this, we were the last to leave the restaurant. We ate our apple pie and drank our coffee in the main restaurant with the chef who continued to tell us about the restaurant's ecofriendly philosophy and success.

******

Short lived return to the Comox Valley

We spent a few more days in Amsterdam visiting our favourite spots and enjoying Emily's company before flying back to Canada. When we arrived at the Vancouver airport, we went through the immigration line to document that we were returning expats. We needed to fill in specific paperwork and be assigned a number to quote when our shipment from Thailand arrived. The repatriation of long-term expats pre-Covid-19 was not very common and the first border guard was not familiar with the necessary paperwork. Confused by our request he consulted a second officer who found the form we needed at the back of the filing cabinet.

The immigration section of the Vancouver international airport was a busy, stressful place. Travelers who had not followed the clearly posted import rules were sent there to explain why they were importing things that were not allowed. Next to us a couple had been caught with fruit and vegetables, as well as some hard to identify animal products in their luggage. The officer calmly put the offending items into a garbage bag while the owners pleaded for them in their native language. Leaving the pandemonium behind, we walked through the airport door to greet Michael's parents.

By following the correct immigration process we did not pay import tax on our furniture and paintings as they were deemed personal goods. Before our shipment from Thailand arrived, we sorted through the possessions stored at my parents since 2004. We had to throw many items away. The plastic parts had degraded over the years. The rest we moved up to our house in Comox.

As we settled into the house, we decided to renovate to create the open spaces we had become used to. We were busy with friends and family in between projects and the summer went by quickly. In September we left for a six-week Italian holiday with my parents. Michael and I chose not to look for work until we returned from this European holiday, which included time in Rome, Florence, Venice, and Ancona. Our savings had supported us while we renovated, but we knew we were going to have to get serious about looking for work when we returned.

******

During our holiday in Italy Michael received an email that impacted our plan to remain in Canada. The director from our school in Chiangmai was now the executive director of a large international school in the United Arab Emirates. He offered Michael the job of technology director as the incumbent had left due to personal reasons. The start date was January.

According to our research the school was accredited by the International Baccalaureate programme and two United Kingdom international curriculum boards. The salary package for Michael was attractive, though we found out later that it should have been significantly more.

Michael's desire to be a technology director overcame any misgivings we had about the school and living in the United Arab Emirates. We trusted the executive director when he said that Ras Al Khaimah Academy would be a good place to advance up the leadership ladder. Our impression was that he wanted our expertise to raise the quality of the teaching and learning offered at the school. Initial I was not teaching, but within a month of Michael accepting his position I was offered a position teaching grade 6 and 9 science classes.

We rented our house and moved our possessions into storage. While our tickets and work visas to the United Arab Emirates were processed, we stayed at my parents. We flew to Dubai on January 1st, 2014, where we were met by the deputy head teacher of the secondary school. He had a strong Scottish accent and his friendliness was contagious. We quickly loaded our luggage, which included our golf clubs, into the back of his car and drove north to our next international experience.

Chapter 5:
United Arab Emirates
2014-2016

*All things are subject to interpretation whichever
interpretation prevails at a given time is a
function of power and not truth.*

-Friedrich Nietzsche-

On arrival in Dubai, we saw western tourists and businessmen mixed with people from Africa and Asia. A high percentage of the travelers were wearing clothing commonly seen in the Middle East and India. Women from India, Pakistan, and Bangladesh wore saris and salwar kameez while the men wore long tunics. The Emirati men wore long loose white garments called kandura as well as the traditional headdress. They were completely covered from head to toe. Arab women wore black abayas and the hijab to cover their hair. Some, but not all, wore the face covering called the burqa.

The population of the United Arab Emirates was an unequal mix of foreign nationals and Emerati. In 2014 eighty-eight percent of the population were immigrants and only twelve percent were Emiratis. Of the immigrants twenty-eight percent were Indian, twelve percent were from Pakistan, and seven percent were Bangladeshi. The remaining expatriates came from Europe and other countries such as Thailand and the Philippines.

The UAE economy relied heavily on foreign workers. Labourers were needed by the construction industry as well as the cement and ceramics factories. The hotel industry hired maids and support staff from the Philippines and Thailand. Most foreign workers were men who sent their wages back to their families in their home countries. Because of this, there was a marked difference (2:1) in the number of men and women living in the country.

The UAE gained independence from the British in 1971. There were seven independent emirates, each ruled by their own Sheikh and government systems. Abu Dhabi was the largest emirate and oil exports supported their economy. Dubai focused on commercial and financial centres. Hundreds of multinational corporations established headquarters there. The emirate of Ras Al Khaimah, where we were headed, had an economy based on cement and ceramic exports.

******

Villas and apartments

The city of Ras Al Khaimah was an hour's drive north of Dubai. We reached it by using a newly completed six lane divided highway. The roads in the United Arab Emirates were straight and in good condition. There was little chance of hitting anything but a stray camel, so cars raced along these highways at high speeds. To deter speeding, cameras were placed at regular intervals and tickets were issued by email to the owner of the car. Speeding tickets could add up and once a year discounts were offered to help those with a high number of tickets.

Highway accidents were common and a large hospital had been built alongside the highway south of the city. Michael and I asked about the odd location and the deputy head teacher told us that an important member of a ruling family had died in an accident at that spot on the highway. The hospital was owned by a Korean conglomerate. It provided emergency services as well as elective surgeries for locals and expatriates.

A large shopping mall signaled that we had entered Al Hamra, a suburb just south of the main city. After driving past the entrance and performing a U-turn we turned into the entrance to a housing complex. Our new home was a villa designed for wealthy expatriates. Huge compared to all our previous school apartments, we initially attributed our good fortune to the fact that Michael was the technology director, but this was not the case. The villa had been rented by his predecessor. In the UAE, rents were paid on a yearly basis. The villa was ours until August, but there was a strong possibility that the school would not continue to support the rental contract, and we would have to move out in six months.

The Al Hamra complex included a shopping mall, villas, and apartment buildings of various sizes, two hotels, and a golf club. The project had been completely engineered out of sand and large rocks. The Waldorf Astoria and the Hilton hotels were built directly on the beachfront to take advantage of the views. The villa housing complexes lined the golf course and the taller Marina apartment buildings at the far end of the development had views of either the ocean or the golf course. There were three story apartment buildings close to the Al Hamra Mall.

These were mainly occupied by the people who worked at the hotels, malls, and other small businesses. Potable water for the development was generated by a desalination plant located by the Marina apartments. The water reclaimed from the sewage processing plant was used to water the golf course.

Our new living space did not have much furniture, just the basics—a bed, couch, dining room table, and one desk. Our contract didn't include a shipping allowance, and we had no intention of buying furniture, so we asked for a second desk from the school. We eventually bought bookshelves and kitchen items from Ikea. They were sold when we left.

The decision to keep our possessions to a minimum was a good thing as in May 2015 human resources informed us that our Al Hamra villa was being sold and we had to move. The school offered us an apartment downtown, but it was too far away from the golf course we had joined. We decided to opt out of the school housing "bubble" and rented an apartment in Mina al Arab, a waterfront community, located halfway between the school and golf club. The Mina al Arab complex offered services like haircutters and restaurants as well as a convenient store within walking distance. The beach was readily accessible, but the daily temperatures were not usually cool enough to go for a comfortable walk.

The coastline of the Persian Gulf was barren rock and the beaches were a popular place to build hotels and residential complexes. Few sea birds and very little seaweed or tidal life could be seen on the shores. This was different from my home on the west coast of British Columbia where multiple species of waterfowl as well as fish, shellfish, seals, sea lions, and orcas lived. There the forest was dotted with the white heads of bald eagles. As I walked along the rocky shore, seaweed, urchins, starfish, and anemones were easily seen through the clear water.

******

Buying a car

On our arrival in the UAE it was obvious that we needed a car. The school was in the city proper while our apartment in Al Hamra was a half hour highway drive away. Many dealerships were located on a stretch of the main highway between the school and our villa in Al Hamra. We were dropped off at the Kia dealership by the assistant head teacher with the plan to take a taxi home after going to a few more dealerships along the road.

The salesperson at the Kia was friendly and we were quite impressed with the cars we saw there. After talking about a few models, we left the showroom and walked to the next dealership. What we had not planned for was that most of the businesses in Ras Al Khaimah took two-to-three-hour afternoon breaks. When we arrived, the dealership was closed. Not having mobile phones, we walked to the side of the road to look for taxis. After five minutes we were getting hot standing in the sun. No taxi had driven by, so we decided to start walking to a strip mall that we could see in the distance rather than suffer heatstroke.

We had walked along the highway for about five minutes when a car pulled over. The driver offered us a ride to a taxi stand. Stopping to help others seemed to be a universal courtesy of people living in harsh climates. I had experienced it growing up in Winnipeg. A collective desire to help people in life-threatening conditions existed at both ends of the spectrum, either +30 or -30 degrees Celsius. Michael and I accepted the ride and it turned out the man's young children were enrolled in our school.

In Thailand we had bought a new car rather than a used car. The used car vendors tended to be there one week and not the next. Often used cars were imported from other countries and had likely been in serious accidents. Plus, parts were likely taken from various makes and models. The cars that Michael had looked at all appeared to have bent frames. Therefore, buying a used car was a gamble.

The only new car we could buy in Chiangmai was a white Toyota Yaris which we bought straight from the showroom without a test drive. Test drives were not allowed as the car would then be classified as used. A used car would not be able to sell for full price. Our Yaris was a small functional car, but it did not have a large trunk. We spent two years removing the long clubs from our golf bags and wedging them into the back of the Yaris. We did not wish to repeat the routine for another two or three years, therefore an ample trunk was one of our criteria for buying a car in the UAE.

We had ruled out buying a used car because the extreme heat was hard on cars. Besides, the locals liked driving into the sand dunes for picnics. We knew this was bad for longevity. After looking at many options we bought a new Kia Sorrento. Having a trunk big enough for our golf bags was a requirement the salesman found amusing, but understandable. He was a genial Syrian who we got to know better over the years when we had the car serviced.

Getting a UAE driver's licences was a requirement, and easy to do. A quick visit to the traffic police department to show them our passports and Canadian licences was all it took. Our new driver's licences were hand delivered to the school.

******

Golfing heaven

Michael and I were members of the Al Hamra golf club. The price of membership was close to four thousand US dollars a year each. As members we could play as many times as we liked provided we booked tee times. The Al Hamra golf course was well maintained. It had flood lights on one nine, which were turned on at dusk. The flood lights allowed us to play after school in the winter months. On weekends we often played eighteen holes with players from around the world. We met some people from Northern Europe during the holiday season and coincidentally played with the same couple from Sweden two years in a row. By the end of a few months Michael and I were well known by the receptionists, as well as by the men in charge of the carts.

Al Hamra employed a golf pro who was originally from Northern England. He was an excellent teacher. His adjustments to my swing fixed my tendency to hit right and added yards to my drive. Michael changed from a beginner into a golfer with purpose and ability. The only reason I beat Michael was the fact that he continued to hit his ball into the bushes and sand traps while I tended to stay on the fairway. We entered our scores into the handicap calculator and my handicap dropped from twenty to eight and Michael's dropped from twenty-six to nine.

We frequently played with an American endocrinologist with Egyptian heritage. He had been hired by the health minister to teach the Emiratis doctors about diabetes. Michael and I liked playing with him as he had a great sense of humor. Mohamed's attitude towards playing golf was the same as ours; it was a good excuse for a walk. He lived in one of the hotels close to the club, and it was easy to arrange to play with him when he was available.

One of the most unforgettable moments at Al Hamra was witnessing a hole in one. We were playing in what bordered on sandstorm conditions with bad visibility. No one in our foursome was playing that well because of the conditions, but we stubbornly decided to finish the round. The eleventh hole was a long par three over water. It was a miracle to get on the green in the best of conditions and on this day we could barely see the hole. Our playing partner's tee shot cleared the water, narrowly missed the sand trap, took a strange bounce off a rock, and rolled straight into the hole.

Catastrophe struck our golfing lifestyle in January of 2016. After having a successful year of golf tours, the owner concluded that the two hundred annual members of the club were costing him money. From his perspective, when members booked times to play it meant that tourists could not book times. Tourists paid a higher green fee than members, so he was losing money when they could not play. Without considering solutions that would benefit both groups he quadrupled the annual membership fee. The fall-out was that all but a handful of the members cancelled their memberships and joined clubs in Dubai.

The second golf course in Ras Al Khaimah was located downtown. Tower Links was shorter in length and had more sand traps or "bunkers" around the greens. Michael and I played it a few times when we first arrived in the UAE and were not that impressed. Two holes were infested by mosquitoes (our least favourite insect) and two other holes had incredibly foul sewage smells wafting up from a nearby construction site.

When membership at the Al Hamra course ceased to be a viable option, we bought a short-term package at Tower Links so that we could play golf until we left for the summer. The mosquitoes were still a plague on the holes by the mangrove swamp, but the sewage smell had been remedied. I tolerated the incredibly decrepit ladies locker room where hot water for showering was not always available.

******

Life in the UAE

Michael and I bought most of our groceries at Spinneys, a supermarket chain located in the mall close to where we lived. Spinneys catered to expats, so we found everything we needed if we were willing to pay the price. Imported fruit and vegetables were very expensive while those grown locally were reasonable. A room designated for pork products had a sign warning Muslims not to enter. The sliding doors opened to an area full of sausages, bacon, and pork chops, as well as sliced meats and pork pies.

Michael and I drove to the shopping malls in Ras Al Khaimah for more Middle Eastern and Asian groceries. The malls contained huge food franchises like those found in North America. They carried bulk sizes of everything as well as the ingredients for curries and other Asian favourites. One of the stores had a deli section and we frequently bought chicken korma and dahls to freeze for our meals during the week.

******

We rarely saw our neighbours in the Ras Al Khaimah villa complex. On the right a group of men would show up occasionally on weekends. A couple lived on the left, but we only saw them a few times and never exchanged hellos. From our bedroom window we noticed that these neighbours had set up an above ground pool and were raising ducks. The cages of ducklings were placed around the circumference of the pool which acted as a sewage catchment system.

Our backyard got increasingly smelly, and Michael decided to complain. We could not personally accuse our neighbor of wrongdoing because we really didn't know the rules about raising ducks in the backyard. To avoid this, Michael submitted a concern to the Al Hamra real-estate office that there was a gas smell coming from our backyard. When the company came to check out our complaint, they immediately noticed the duck farm. The maintenance worker did not say anything out loud, but they must have called someone that had influence with our neighbor—the duck operation was shut down once the birds were harvested.

******

While out buying an inexpensive carpet to put on our tile floors Michael and I found a traditional Indian restaurant located on a small road filled with potholes. The restaurant was not large or glamourous. The decor was a flashback to traveling in northern India. Plastic tablecloths covered the tables and the glasses and plates were stainless steel. We recognized the names of foods listed on the English menu and ordered our favourite dishes. The exclusively vegetarian dishes were as tasty as the ones we had enjoyed in northern India and Bangladesh. We returned to enjoy the food on a regular basis.

Michael and I would eat at restaurants one or two times a week. There was never a shortage of places to go. On Fridays we ate at the Belgium Café located next to the Al Hamra golf range. A speciality beer and burger were our usual order though they had other options on the menu. The main golf club house had a more formal Italian restaurant, a bar, as well as a coffee shop. The coffee shop served waffles and English breakfasts. Other options for food near our house included the food court at the Al Hamra Mall where the main Middle Eastern, Chinese, and western fast-food chains had outlets. Just outside the food court was a sushi chain, which served a variety of rolls that kept us returning for more.

One of our favourite places to eat in Ras Al Khaimah was the Cove Rotana. Located halfway between our Al Hamra villa resort and the city of Ras Al Khaimah it was a beautiful resort with a hotel as well as beachfront villas. The restaurant at the Cove had excellent food and very good service. Their signature menu items were salmon under glass and lamb chops. Side orders of tabbouleh and hummus were exceptional — I have not eaten anything to match the quality of their hummus anywhere else in the world. The entrance to the Cove was a façade of an old castle wall. Originally it was built to let only one car through at a time. As traffic became more congested, they rebuilt the entrance to allow two cars to drive in and out at the same time.

For pizza and pasta we went to the Thunder Road Pizza and Grill owned by Italian expatriates. Like Pern's in Thailand the owners had not been able to afford opening a restaurant in their home country, so had started one in the UAE. Located in a small strip mall on the way from Al Hamra to the city the building was easy to miss as there was no obvious access road off the highway. Turning into and out of the restaurant was always nerve racking as the traffic was traveling at 100 km/hr. The amazing pizzas were made in a traditional oven and it was a popular expat hang-out. On one occasion the owner made fresh buffalo mozzarella cheese in front of us. He then added this fresh cheese to our salads. The Thunder Road take-out menu supported Michael during our year apart.

******

The air temperature in the Middle East rose to 50° in the summer months and only dipped to lows of 10-15 ° in the winter. Air conditioning units were essential for those coming from northern climates. Michael and I had experienced hot and humid weather in Thailand, as well as Bangladesh, so we were not as badly affected by the heat as our United Kingdom colleagues. I carried a hand fan with me to create my own evaporating wind in Bangladesh, Thailand, and the United Arab Emirates, but did not need it in South Korea.

There were similarities to living in extremely hot and extremely cold climates. Growing up in Winnipeg, Manitoba, I lived in one of the coldest cities in the world. In the downtown core networks of tunnels and overhead walkways were specifically designed so that people did not have to walk outside. Forty degrees below zero (-40 °C) with a wind chill making it comparable to -85°C was not pleasant. Frostbite warnings on public radio stations would warn residents about the length of time needed for exposed skin to freeze. Sometimes it would be only a few minutes. Everyone had to dress appropriately.

On the other side of the temperature scale the Middle East was extremely hot. All the major malls and shops in the United Arab Emirates were air conditioned. They were also connected to the transit system with tunnels and walkways. Michael and I very rarely walked outside when we lived there. Temperatures were usually above 25° except in late December and January. Walking the short distance from the car to the entrance of the mall was enough time to start sweating.

******

Dubai had some of the biggest shopping malls in the world. Each mall had a specific attraction. One had a huge aquarium; another had a ski slope and ice rink, while a third was located besides the tallest building in the world, the Burj Khalifa. Michael and I liked the mall with the Ikea store. It was the closest one to our house and further away from the center of town, so it was not as full of tourists.

Michael and I did not drive to Dubai very often as it was nerve racking. Many Emirati drivers were aggressive and treated the road like it belonged to them. In bumper to bumper traffic these aggressive drivers would flash their lights and drive up as close as possible to make you get out of the way. This behaviour caused accidents. Like in Moscow and Thailand the foreign driver was held responsible—if the foreigner had not been there, there would not have been an accident.

Adding to the stress of aggressive drivers was the fact that navigating in Dubai was difficult. The signage was confusing. Roads would split before the GPS told us which fork to take. The aerial multi-lane traffic circles were a real challenge and Michael did a lot of backtracking and swearing. The pace of development did not help as frequently the GPS thought we were in the middle of a field when in fact we were driving through in a new subdivision.

Dubai was a city full of hotels, malls, and restaurants. A nursing friend from Comox and her husband worked in Saudi at the same time we were in the UAE. We arranged to meet them at the ski hill mall when they were in Dubai for a shopping holiday. We ate lunch at a sushi restaurant located at the bottom of the indoor ski hill. The experience was surreal as it was over 30° outside and people were skiing down an artificial ski slope. The amount of energy to produce the artificial snow would have been enormous.

Another time we met friends from Moscow at a Brazilian meat restaurant called Fogo de Chao for dinner. The meal was worth the hassle of finding the restaurant amongst the skyscrapers. There was a set fee for dinner. After choosing our salad from the salad bar the rest of the meal was meat. Waiters carried skewers of barbecued pork, beef, and lamb between tables. They cut off tasty pieces of the perfectly cooked meat and placed them on our plates. At the beginning of the meal, we were given a coaster with a green side and a red side. The green side signaled the waiters to continue to bring meat. The red side told them we were finished. We all ate a lot of meat that night. Good beef and lamb were hard to find in Ras Al Khaimah. It was a real treat.

******

Holidays — Musandam, Oman

On one of our earlier holidays Michael and I drove to Musandam, a governorate of Oman. We had not expected the small border crossing between Ras Al Khaimah and Musandam to be busy, but it was. The room was literally overflowing with people, and being processed out of the United Arab Emirates took an hour. Next, we crossed to the other side to be stamped into Oman where it took the same amount of time to get through. We had been told to take a pen which was good advice—the one pen in the room was being shared by forty people. Eventually we got through and started the scenic drive up the coastal road to Khasab. The road wound along the base of sandstone mountains sloping steeply down to meet the turquoise ocean.

Musandam offered traditional Dhow cruises. These tours took tourists through the fjords of the peninsula to the historic islet called Telegraph Island. Michael and I enjoyed a half day dhow tour. The boat motored slowly between the islands in the marine park. We were lucky enough to see a pod of endangered pink porpoises. When the dolphins were spotted our boat was joined by many other tourist boats. It got crowded and I worried about the effect on the dolphins. The boat stopped for an hour at Telegraph Island where Michael snorkeled with other members of our group to see the tropical fish and other sea life living in the corals.

******

Teaching at RAK Academy

Unlike our previous schools, RAK Academy was a large organization with over three thousand students from kindergarten to grade twelve. Three separate schools housed multiple classes of each grade and hundreds of teachers. A four-member appointed school board ran the organization and their actions were overseen by the Sheikh. The executive director had been hired directly by the Sheikh and he followed the directions given by the board.

New teachers were invited by the Sheikh of Ras Al Khaimah to his mountain house at the beginning of each year. Getting there was an adventure; four-wheel drive vehicles were necessary to drive the last few kilometers. The small complex had been built before the road had been completed. This meant that all the materials had been flown in using helicopters. The courtyard provided amazing views of the ocean. Close by there was an experimental garden of orange and lemon trees.

While we sat in a circle drinking tea and eating dates, the Sheikh spoke to us enthusiastically about the importance of education and the role of foreign teachers in his plan for Ras Al Khaimah. An intelligent man, he knew that future generations of Emirati children needed to be educated to fill the middle-class occupations currently occupied by expatriates. Oil reserves in Abu Dhabi were running out and this meant that the days of dividend income were coming to an end—a shift in thinking that required Emirati children to successfully complete post-secondary education programs.

The student population at RAK Academy was predominantly from the Persian Gulf states with students from the Emirates as well as Egypt, Yemen, and Syria. Coming from a mixture of backgrounds most of the Emirati families were connected to the wealth and power of the country's businesses established in the 1950s. One of my middle school students showed me a picture of his new racing camel calf worth half a million dollars. These Emirati students did not see the need to attend university to improve their social position. The value of education and there-fore the attitude towards learning was very different compared to European and North American students.

RAK Academy used a British curriculum. The students wrote external exams in grades ten and eleven. In 2014 Emirati students did not need to pass external UK exams to move forward to the local universities. All that was required was an attendance record from kindergarten to grade eleven. Most of the senior, sixth form (grade 11) class had been advanced without passing grade ten exams. They attended one or two grade eleven classes and spent the rest of the day in the common room. The students wrote the end of year exams, but failing did not impact their future posi-tions in the family businesses. Only a handful of Emirati students completed grade twelve and pursued university degrees overseas.

In 2015 the Sheikh made the decision that Emirati students were required to pass two external board exams if they wanted to continue to university and avoid military service.

The new directive was a major challenge for the secondary school. Emirati children were intelligent and capable, but many did not have the study skills to attain high academic grades internally or externally. Successful study skills and revision plans were not part of their cultural experience. Their great-grandparents had been nomadic traders, fishermen or pearl divers before the oil boom of the 1960's. Few parents and grandparents had completed grade twelve or attended university. Therefore, they knew little about the routines needed for academic success.

When I arrived my middle school classes were completely disruptive. I initiated multiple classroom management strategies and looked seriously at the reasons why the students were so disruptive. I found that many students did not understand the concept that they were there to learn and that education was important. For them school was a place to play with their friends. It did not help that the majority of the students did not understand half of what I was saying in English. The English language support team had been dismantled the year before which was not helpful in a school where the mother tongue was Arabic. After making fundamental changes to lessons, my students started to understand what was expected of them and they began to enjoy learning.

******

The science teachers at RAK Academy were supported by three technicians who brought lab equipment and chemicals to the rooms when requested. The most senior technician had a degree in pharmacy and the other two were completely subservient to her. They did not have science backgrounds. The chemical storage rooms at RAK Academy were an extreme example of people in power not understanding the dangers of storing toxic, explosive, and carcinogenic chemicals. The odor of volatile organics was stronger than what I had encountered in Thailand. In fact, the chemical storage room was a disaster waiting to happen. Chemical spills had discolored and eroded the shelves and it was evident that nothing had been cleaned for years. Bottle labels were not legible due to corrosion. In many cases crystals of the liquid chemicals could be seen on the outside due to bad pouring techniques. The single storage cabinet for explosive chemicals had rusted doors and was not clean. The excuse the pharmacist gave for not cleaning and maintaining this area was that it was not her job.

I asked the head of science why the room was not meeting the safety standards of chemical storage. He shrugged his shoulders and seemed to be okay with the situation. He informed me that a request for a ventilation fan had been put in the previous year. No fan had appeared with the "inshallah" (God willing) attitude for things that do not get done. That was the end of the conversation. A fan was only one of many things that needed to be addressed in that room. It was a toxic wasteland and I had no power to remedy the situation.

Changes to the chemical storage room occurred when the school did not pass the health and safety criteria required by the Council of International Schools to receive accreditation status. The school hired a firm to correct the issues and the chemical storage room was immediately locked. The technicians did not fully understand why the room had been locked and wanted to continue to eat their lunches in there. The idea that the toxic air in the prep room could cause cancers was not part of their ethos. Over the next few weeks a large portion of the chemicals were disposed of, proper cabinets were bought, new shelves were purchased, and a fan system was installed.

******

Snake in the Grass — time to move on

My work experiences in Canada, Moscow, Bangladesh, and Thailand had not prepared me for the unprofessional behaviours I experienced at RAK Academy. Many of the high school teachers viewed student-centered teaching practices as impractical and too much work. My desire to improve the learning experiences of students was threatening and my student-focussed projects were the brunt of jokes.

Academic honesty was a requirement for external UK exams given at the end of grade 10, 11, and 12. The security of exam papers was the role of the exams officer and strict invigilation processes were expected to be followed to prevent cheating. The validity of the exams was paramount to the university selection process, but due to historical data university admission teams around the world were skeptical of the results from the Middle East and with good reason.

Invigilators were frequently on their phones, and not watching the students. A group of students were caught one year when the exam board found a consistent pattern in their answers. The students had been seated close together and had used hand signals to convey the multiple-choice answers. Ironically the answers had not been right, but consistently wrong.

There was also a pattern in which students who failed all their grade ten exams magically attained good scores in a specific subject in their grade eleven exams. The passing grades could have been achieved by studying, but the difference between the scores was extreme and the results repeated over years. The pattern suggested that a tutor had access to the exam questions and was able to coach their clients to a passing grade.

Unaware of possible ramifications I insisted that I be involved in the running of the mock and final exams. Separate from the UK exams, I coordinated a small cohort of students taking the International Baccalaureate program exams. I took my role seriously and I wanted to make sure that these exams were done following the exam writing guidelines. I cleaned up the exam room of any excess envelops and increased the accountability of invigilators during the mock exams. I had no idea my actions would result in my removal from my coordinator role and from teaching high school classes. The person who needed access to the questions did not appreciate the tightening of security and they had friends in powerful places. The plot to remove me from teaching high school classes and coordinating the international baccalaureate program began in January.

My nemesis used students who I did not teach to write a letter accusing me of poor teaching practices. Co-workers and fellow conspirators who benefited from my removal as coordinator openly participated in supporting the lies. My adversary was always friendly and supportive to my face and I was unable to confirm their identity until years later. I was helpless against these false accusations which went straight to the board. The executive director, head teacher, and deputy head were more concerned about their continued employment than my professional credibility. They did nothing to counter the lies—it appeared to me they believed them.

The process of undermining my credibility took eight months of lies and gossip fed to the chairman of the board, the ministry, and ultimately to the Sheikh. Finally, the poor exam results of the grade eleven cohorts were blamed on me, even though the small cohort of students that I did have control over all passed. The accusation was ludicrous, and I was powerless to do anything to counter it. I was told by the executive director in the presence of the head and deputy head that I was removed from my teaching position, as well as the coordinator role, by direct order of the Sheikh. It was the first day of the new school year.

The executive director, who we had considered a friend, did not warn me of what was coming when we had dinner the night before, though he must have known. Although I had been hired by this man to positions in three international schools, he did nothing to support me. His actions were unforgiveable and a complete betrayal of my trust.

My last year in Ras Al Khaimah was extremely stressful as I tried to figure out who my enemy was, what had really happened, as well as why. The school could not find a replacement teacher at such short notice. I continued teaching my middle school science classes and one grade 12 psychology class. The coordinator role was given to the assistant head teacher. I struggled with the fact that my credibility and reputation as a teacher had not been defended by people I considered friends. I obviously did not fit into the schools teaching milieu. When I was offered only middle school science classes for the following year I resigned.

******

Within a few weeks of making myself available on the hiring databases, I received an email from the high school principal at Branksome Hall Asia. She was looking for an IBDP biology teacher. A well-respected international baccalaureate school, its vision and mission resonated with my values. I was well qualified to teach high school biology, as well as middle school science. After a brief second interview with the director I was offered the position.

I was excited and looking forward to working with people who had the same professional goals as I had. The problem was that there was no position for Michael. The only available vacancy was a combination of higher-level math and design technology. Michael was okay with the design technology part, but not the higher-level math. Besides, he still had projects he wanted to complete in his role as technology director at RAK academy.

We had two choices. One was for Michael to ask if he could continue at RAK Academy and we would work separately for a year. The second was for Michael to be a "trailing spouse," which was potentially going to be boring and not financially viable. After much discussion, separation for a year seemed like a feasible idea. The director agreed to have Michael continue as Technology Director to complete the projects he had started.

My ability to trust the intent of others at face value was significantly damaged. This experience raised my awareness of the importance of organizational systems and the intent of those who work within them. The worst consequence of the actions of everyone involved was that my husband and I lived apart for the next school year.

*****

Chapter 6:
Jeju Island, South
Korea 2016-2021

*Getting ready for my new adventure in Branksome Hall
Asia, Jeju Island, Korea teaching IBDP Biology! Michael
and I are going to experience the "work in different
countries" lifestyle. Never a dull moment for us.*

-Facebook post 2016-

South Korean work visa—not as easy as we thought

After signing my contract, I started the process of getting a South
Korean work visa. One of the required documents was a recent
criminal record check from Canada, which was surprising as
we had not lived there for twelve years. Criminal record checks
were obtained from the Royal Canadian Mounted Police with
proof of residency, but we were not in Canada. Waiting to return
to Canada for our summer holidays would not give the South

Korean government time to process my work visa before the school year started.

Michael searched the Internet and found a company that offered criminal record checks to Canadians living abroad. After a few false starts we were informed that residents of British Columbia were required to supply fingerprints for the criminal record check; this was different from other provinces. We downloaded and printed the required forms, then organized a time to get my fingerprints taken at the main police station in Ras Al Khaimah.

The police station in Ras Al Khaimah was an improvement on the police station we had visited in Dhaka after our early morning assault. The entrance was clean and manned by a well-dressed officer. After signing in at the front desk we were taken down a dark windowless hallway lined with large, barred prison cells full of men who did not look very happy. The Supervisor's office was at the end of the hallway; it was well lit and full of comfortable couches and chairs.

The Supervisor spoke very little English. Initially he was not sure what we needed. After some miming and slow explanations, he understood and all my ten digits were printed in the correct places using copious amounts of ink. The Supervisor merrily stamped the document in the places he was supposed to. We thanked him profusely, paid him for his time, and drove to the FedEx office.

We couriered my fingerprint documents to the company in Canada where they were processed by the Royal Canadian Mounted Police in British Columbia. The completed document were returned back to the school and then forwarded to the South Korean visa office. This part of the visa process took a month and we were glad to have it completed.

My teaching credentials were copied and apostilled by a lawyer in Canada. We had couriered the original documents to a friend in Victoria. Her lawyer made notarized copies which were sent along with a letter of authenticity signed by the lawyer to the South Korean Embassy in Vancouver. These copies were couriered back to our friend in Victoria and she forwarded them to the school in Jeju. Michael and I collected the original documents when we returned to Canada that summer.

The day after we arrived back in Canada, I gave my passport to the South Korean Embassy in Vancouver. We had done everything as quickly as possible. Even with everything going smoothly I received my work visa and passport two days before I flew to Jeju Island to start my new job.

******

Branksome Hall Asia

In the early 2000s the South Korean government brainstormed new initiatives to promote economic growth. The politicians agreed to create a "Free International City" as a base for new international businesses on Jeju Island. In 2002 the Jeju Free International City Development Center (JDC) was formed by a special act of government. The JDC was a public corporation controlled by the Ministry of Land, Infrastructure, and Transport.

Megaprojects like the Shinwa Amusement Park and hotel complexes were built around Jeju Island. These projects created opportunities for business and stimulated the economy. An important part of the JDC initiative was the creation of the Global Education City (GEC). A large section of rural land was designated to accommodate five international schools, a preschool, and eight apartment complexes. The plans included designated spaces for food stores, restaurants, doctors' offices, and other businesses.

A self-contained city, the GEC offered international educational opportunities to Korean parents. The development addressed the fact that large numbers of Koreans were sending their children overseas to obtain an education in English. Fathers remained working in South Korea while their wives and children moved to North America or the United Kingdom to attend school. According to government records available on the internet, in 2009 $4.46 billion US dollars were being spent overseas because of this practice.

The Korean government wished to keep the money in Korea and decrease the emotional cost to families. To reach their goal the JDC negotiated with major international private k-12 schools to build schools on Jeju Island. North London Collegiate School (UK) and Branksome Hall Asia (Canada) were the first to be built in the Global Education City (GEC), opening their doors in 2012. St. Johnsbury Academy Jeju (USA) opened in 2017. A sister school of the Korea International School (KIS) in Seoul was built. KIS followed an American curriculum but, because it was Korean owned, it did not have the same levels of bureaucracy that existed for Branksome Hall, North London Collegiate School, and St. Johnsbury. There were rumours of a sister school of one of international schools in Shanghai, but it was not built when I lived on Jeju Island.

The GEC was successful. By 2021 the schools enrolled thousands of students. Graduates were accepted by universities around the world, as well as within Korea. All schools offered boarding services, but families often rented or bought apartments in the newly built apartment blocks surrounding the schools. Businesses and restaurants filled the retail spaces. Within a decade, the area became a bustling community.

Teachers who started at Branksome Hall Asia in 2012 saw the vision materialize. They told stories of living in the first apartment complex with only one small convenience store, called the "CU," for emergency food and drink. The planned community grew from nothing but forest and rocks. When I arrived on Jeju Island in 2016 three large apartment complexes existed, with two more near completion. Two small organic groceries stores were within walking distance and a Paris Baguette provided bread and treats. The original CU had been joined by a second convenience store called GS25. More importantly, a Starbucks opened just outside our school's gates. Choices for eating out included Italian, Thai, and deep-fried chicken restaurants located in strip malls beside NLCS and Branksome Hall Asia.

When I first arrived, my friend Toni and I drove half an hour to the closest town to buy basic supplies. This included more substantial amounts of fruits, vegetables, and meat. Not surprisingly, western products like cheese and sausages were not available in the small towns. When shopping we used our international experiences to decipher pictures and guess what the packages contained. When that did not work, we turned to technology. A downloaded translation app helped us find salt and baking powder. For western foods we traveled to Emart and Lotte Mart located in the larger cities of Seogwipo and Jeju city. Toni and I saved these excursions for the weekends as the cities were at least an hour away depending on traffic conditions.

By 2021 the GEC complex was almost complete. The planned retail complexes at the base of the development were finished. The new businesses included a third organic food store as well as a large Korean supermarket. Dentists, dermatologists, doctors, and pharmacies had opened their doors within the various allotted spaces. Hairdressers and nail salons as well as screen golf and bakeries quickly followed. More high-end restaurants opened as well as wine and liquor stores. By the time I left Branksome Hall Asia there was no need to venture far from home.

******

Things to do on Jeju

In the fall of 2016, the school hired Michael as a full-time design technology teacher to start in August 2017. As 2016 turned into 2017 Michael and I found it very difficult to live apart. An arrangement was made with RAK Academy whereby Michael came to Korea in April. He worked online from Jeju until June, at which time he returned to the United Arab Emirates to pack up his remaining personal items before meeting me in Canada.

Michael and I appreciated the rural atmosphere, clean air, and lack of traffic noise on Jeju Island. It was mainly a farming community—great for nature lovers, hikers, and cyclists. The island was designated a UNESCO Natural Heritage Site. Hiking trails climbed the dormant volcano Halla Mountain and wound around the outlying small volcanic hills called oreums. These trails were very popular with Korean and Chinese tourists. We frequently saw hikers wearing new hiking clothes bought especially for these walks. Other places of interest were the volcanic lava tube and Sunrise Peak on the most easterly point of Jeju.

In addition to the trails up the volcano and oreums there were twenty-six official walking trails called Olle trails. Olle trails combined small access roads with trails up the oreums. They had been inspired by the Camino de Santiago pilgrimage in Spain. The system circumnavigated the island highlighting the volcanic features and history of the areas. The only drawback was that the trails were one-way. Hikers needed to coordinate how they were going to get back to their starting point by using friends, tour companies, taxis or the bus system or be prepared to walk the trail in reverse. Many of our teaching friends completed all the Olle trails. They collected stamps from the tourist offices located along the trails to fill their Olle booklet. Michael and I were not serious hikers. We did not officially start or finish any walks, but we did walk up oreums and along parts of many of the trails on our side of the island.

Jeju was a major tourist destination. The incredibly efficient airport was one of the busiest airports in the world. Tourists would travel to the island at specific times to be photographed in fields of yellow canola flowers or white pampas grass; or they would seek beaches for sunrise and sunset photographs. Toni and I found this amusing, especially when the owners of the fields would charge a dollar for parking on the side of the public road in front of their field. Regardless of the charge I could understand why the fields were so attractive to people living in big cities. They were beautiful.

******

My first year on Jeju was spent in the company of my friends who I had originally met in Moscow—Kate, Kerry and Toni. Kate and Kerry lived in the same apartment complex as me and Toni was just down the road. Toni rented a car when she arrived and I joined her when she drove to the larger cities.

Living on Jeju Island was like returning to Russia—few local islanders understood English and many spoke a local dialect distinct to Jeju. The language barrier made it difficult for us to go to hair salons in the local town. I tried once, but was unsuccessful and was never brave enough to try again.

To get our hair cut and colored Toni and I drove to Kevin's salon in Jeju city. Recommended by a friend, Kevin had trained in the United Kingdom and knew how to cut curly hair. We used Facebook to book appointments. A day trip, our haircuts were combined with buying food at Martro or E-mart and going for lunch.

When Toni took a job in Saudi Arabia I used the new translation app to make appointments at the hair salons which had opened closer to the GEC. The advantage of trying these places was that I did not have to drive to Jeju city and battle the ever-increasing traffic. The downside was that none of the haircuts were as good as Kevin's—the stylists were not as experienced. When Covid-19 lockdowns began, I stopped going to hairdressers and let my natural grey hair grow.

******

Business hours on Jeju Island were irregular. Restaurants could be closed any day of the week and the smaller places had long lunch breaks. Unusual opening hours also occurred at the large chain stores like Emart and Lotte Mart which closed every second Friday and every fourth Saturday of the month. We were mostly caught out on Saturdays; we kept forgetting these unusual hours of operation. We frequently arrived at an empty parking lot and would look at each other with disgust and say in unison, "closed every second Friday and every fourth Saturday." To stop this stupid behaviour, we began shopping on Sundays.

******

Jeju Island had regular open markets in the cities, but the small towns had markets that ran on a five-day cycle. The market close to us was known for its fish selection, but you could find pretty much anything there. Cheap clothing, expensive traditionally dyed clothing, blankets, vegetables, meat, fish, seeds, farming equipment, medicinal herbs, flowers, live chickens, and puppies. The markets were full of locals doing their weekly shopping as well as tourists walking down the aisles witnessing the wonders of a traditional marketplace. I liked looking at the variety of things for sale, though usually just bought plants or seeds and stayed away from the fresh produce and meat—I did not know enough Korean to barter.

******

Korean Driver's License

When Michael and I flew to South Korea in 2016 we spent a few days exploring Seoul before continuing on to Jeju. The layover allowed us to recover from jet lag, do some sightseeing in Seoul as well as acquire the paperwork needed for Korean driver's licenses. We visited the Canadian Embassy and paid fifty dollars for a document officially stating that our Canadian driver's licenses were valid. The Transportation Office licensing department on Jeju Island needed the Canadian embassy form, our Canadian licences, as well as a signed letter from the Global Education City office stating that we were residents of Jeju.

After handing over the documents the licencing clerk gave us multiple forms to fill out. They were in Korean, but an accompanying translation book helped us fill in all the boxes. The questions related to health and wellness and our ability to drive.

Once the forms were completed, we took a five-dollar eye test which was entertaining. The tester did not speak English and the chart had symbols not letters. I assumed that they knew the words for dog, duck, and tractor. If not, they passed me just because it looked like I could see something on the chart. With everything in order, we received Korean licences.

Our Canadian licences were returned when we showed our return plane tickets to Canada. At this point in my life I had drivers' licenses for the United Arab Emirates, Canada, and Korea in my wallet. Sadly, my ten-year-old Russian license, which had taken the whole day to acquire, had expired.

******

Buying a car

Michael and I bought a car on Jeju Island — there was a strong possibility that we would work at Branksome Hall Asia for three to five years. The GEC was not close to towns or cities and we did not want to rely on our friends with cars or public transit. Renting cars long term was a common choice of teachers, but Michael calculated that buying was a better financial choice in the long run.

Michael looked at used cars with the "Queen of Jeju." An American, she had lived on Jeju Island for years and spoke Korean. She made a living out of helping expatriates buy used cars in Jeju city. Michael's distrust of the reliability of a used car had not abated and we decided to buy new. We asked the school's human resources department to help us find a dealer. Coincidentally the man in charge of buses and transportation had an uncle who owned a Hyundai dealership.

Michael and I looked at brochures after doing some internal research. The uncle came to the school and using his nephew to translate we discussed models and prices. We could only afford the Hyundai Avanti so picked that one on the brochure. The uncle told us that the only color available was silver unless we wanted to wait for three months. Silver and white cars were the norm in Korea. Since we wanted the car immediately, we chose silver. The dealership accepted our cash deposit and we used our visa card for the remainder of the price. Our new silver Hyundai Avanti was delivered to the school's front entrance after we bought car insurance over the phone.

We drove the Avanti for four years and never had trouble with maintenance or breakdowns. The cars computer systems would warn us if the tire pressure was low and if anything else needed to be checked. Our friend Xenia bought it from us when we left Branksome Hall Asia and appreciated the upgrade from her smaller car.

******

Apartment living

When I started at Branksome Hall Asia I was assigned a single bedroom apartment. On the main floor of a three-story apartment building, it had a large window and patio door which looked over a green forest. I liked my apartment, but when Michael was hired I requested a larger one. The school was happy to do this and all my possessions were moved to a three-bedroom couple's apartment located a bit closer to school. It was a stress-free move. Movers arrived, packed everything, drove to the new apartment, and unpacked everything the way they had found it in the first apartment.

Unfortunately, the new apartment was not that wonderful. Increased space did not compensate for noisy neighbours. A couple with a screaming toddler moved in above us. As the screaming stopped the running back and forth increased; I'm not sure which was worse. As the apartment was on the main floor, our living room and bedroom windows faced directly onto parking lots. We had little privacy. Finding parking spots became increasingly difficult as the vacant apartments filled up with tenants. When the human resources department offered teachers the opportunity to live outside the Global Education City boundaries, we decided to look at the possibilities.

Serendipitously we found a brochure advertising the purchase or rental of brand new, single family dwellings while we were eating at a sushi restaurant. The development had sixteen small identical houses located on a hill overlooking fields of cabbages and broccoli. The houses were only a fifteen-minute drive from the school. We drove to see the complex and conveniently the owner/designer of the houses was there finishing up some of the finer details. Able to communicate with us in broken English he told us that two of the houses were available for rent. With the help of the school, we negotiated a two year rental contract within a few weeks of seeing the houses.

Living away from the school was peaceful. I never tired of the view over the fields. The house was about half the size of the apartment, but it was a single-family unit and had no shared walls. The complex was quiet and we rarely saw our neighbours. Koreans did not seem to have the same need for "neighbourly" interactions as Canadians and the language barrier was a deterrent. A friend gave us a charcoal smoker to put in our backyard.

Over the next two years Michael perfected the technique of smoking pork, chicken, and fish.

While living outside the GEC bubble we were able to enjoy the rural nature of Jeju Island. Pheasants could be heard every day and the farmers planted the fields with a variety of crops depending on the four growing seasons. Michael and I would try to guess what each one was as the plants started to grow. Beets, corn, wheat, barley, cabbage, onions, garlic, and sesame seeds were all successfully grown in our area. Michael and I walked down the country lanes without worrying about being hit by cars though the farm trucks tended to travel at incredible speeds and did not always stop at intersections.

******

Golfing

When we researched Jeju Island on the internet, we saw that there were more than twenty golf courses. We were hopeful that we could continue playing like we had in Ras Al Khaimah. On further investigation we found that the green fees were astronomical and a yearly membership was completely out of the question. You had to be making significantly more than a teacher to belong to Korean private golf clubs.

Finding time to play at the public courses was challenging. We did not usually leave the school until five o'clock on weekdays. Weekends in August and September were hot and humid, as well as being typhoon season. In the winter it was dark and cold. The weather improved in the spring, but marking papers and preparing students for their final exams took priority. When we found time, it was difficult to communicate with the golf courses to set up tee times. In the five years I lived on Jeju Island I played on golf courses less than ten times.

To maintain our skills Michael and I played screen golf. A big business in Korea, screen golf franchises offered lessons for children and adults as well as special rooms which could be booked for private groups. We found one we liked close to the school. The rooms were set up with computer systems that simulated golf courses on Jeju and around the world.

Screen golf was a lot of fun, but I did not take it too seriously as it was very different from playing on a real course. We were joined by fellow golfing addicts from school and it was one of the things we did for entertainment after school and on weekends. Michael and I took my father to our usual screen golf place when he came to visit. He was quite impressed with the system and we all had a good laugh playing the virtual Pebble Beach course.

******

Utility bills and car inspection

Functioning in a society where we did not speak read or write the language was a skill we mastered over the years. Shopping for food had its challenges. The process for paying bills was more interesting depending on the country we lived in. We had no utility bills in Moscow as the schools housing department looked after all bills and repairs. The same was true for Bangladesh and Thailand. We relearned how to pay utility invoices when we returned to Canada for six months. Technology advances had created online banking services in Canada and these services were available in Korea. Korean utility companies had a system of direct deposit for their invoices and all we needed to find was the number for the account on the invoice. The system was so precise that we could only transfer the exact amount on the invoice. When we received unusual invoices in our mailbox, we asked the human resource department to help us find the appropriate account number to pay into.

The invoices we received at the apartments were large folding documents which included graphs of energy and water usage over time. A colleague spent the time translating the information on this document and found it humorous that an elevator maintenance fee was included even though she lived on the first floor. The strata fee was one of the downsides of living in the apartment complex.

Every once in a while, something new would appear. In March of 2021 I received a Korean text message from an unknown caller. The message could have been several things including advertising spam, but I decided to translate it using my translation app. The message was a request to register my car for its mandatory inspection. Car inspections were required by law depending on the age of the car and as ours was four years old it needed its first one.

Michael went to the Korean website. It had a partial translation into English which was helpful, but when we pushed the link to book a time the page was in Korean. Using his phone app to translate the important parts of the webpage Michael managed to book an appointment on the upcoming Friday. He paid for the appointment and downloaded the receipt as well as the appointment booking slip using the translation app. After printing the documents, we pinned the location of the inspection office in Jeju city.

We hoped the Korean papers in the glove compartment were the ownership papers, but there was no way to tell for sure. We knew that the car's insurance papers were in order— we placed them in the glove compartment every year. At the inspection station the inspector asked for our papers in Korean. We handed him the folder; he picked out the correct document and placed it on the dashboard.

The inspection was an assembly line. We watched what other drivers did and followed them. Inspections of brakes, emissions, and lights were completed as the car proceeded along the line while we waited in a room at the end. When our car arrived at the end an inspector told us in broken English that we had "passed" and we did not have to come back for two years. He put a sticker on the registration document which we returned to the glove compartment. We drove away happy to have negotiated the car inspection without speaking any Korean.

******

Eating out on Jeju Island

I first experienced the hot-pot method of cooking food while living on Jeju. A propane powered hotplate was placed in the middle of the table and a large pot of broth filled with various uncooked ingredients was placed on it. The waiter turned on the stove. We watched as the broth came to a boil and cooked the meat and vegetables. Once the food had cooked, we took turns filling our bowls from the main pot and added condiments and spices found on the table. Cooking this way was simple provided everything was cut the same size.

Korean barbecues were a unique experience. Various cuts of meat were cooked over hot coals in a brazier set in the middle of the table. A grill was fitted on top of the coals, and the raw meat was brought out on a plate. A vacuum extractor tube hung above the brazier to collect the smoke that came from the meat as it cooked. Meat strips were put on whole and then flipped and cut into smaller pieces using tongs and large scissors. Scissors were a common utensil in Korean kitchens as they were used to cut noodles, meat, and vegetables. If the vacuum was not placed properly the restaurant would fill with smoke and the waiter would run over to rectify the situation while "tut-tutting" and shaking their head. I knew they were thinking "silly foreigners", but in a friendly, helpful way.

Beef and pork barbecue restaurants offered multiple side dishes which were included in the price of the meal. These small plates were refilled on demand. We did not recognize some of the contents, but most were edible. Whole blue crabs were not a favourite of mine, but our friend Emily chewed them up with great abandon when she came to visit. The side dishes covered the table and there was no room for a personal dinner plate. The correct way to eat Korean barbecue was to wrap the cooked meat with the condiments inside lettuce leaves, like a Mexican burrito. Very few restaurants provided forks and knives. Everything was cut with scissors and eaten with chopsticks.

One time Toni and I ventured into a newly opened barbeque restaurant. When we were shown to our table it was apparent that the server did not understand English. Luckily the menus had pictures of the meat dishes that could be ordered. Toni and I decided to share a lovely looking pork barbeque selection and a beef bulgogi soup.

We signaled the server that we were ready to order. We pointed at the pork selection and put up one finger, and then pointed to the bulgogi selection and put up one finger. He shook his head, put up two fingers, and in very broken English said we had to order two. This confused us. It made no sense that we had to order four servings, but the server was not able to explain the rationale. We agreed to the two orders of pork, but insisted that we only wanted one order of the soup.

The server seemed to understand our signing and pointing and headed off to the kitchen. Within five minutes a man who was obviously the cook came to our table and with aggressive sign language indicated that we had to have two servings of both. We were a bit taken aback by this turn of events, quickly apologized for our ignorance, and agreed to whatever they thought was best.

I found out later that the cook made enough for two when you ordered one dish. This was a culture of sharing and when going to a Korean barbeque we had to be willing to eat a lot of food. In truth, the main social event while living in Korean was eating out with friends, so this was not an issue.

******

We found that the restaurants in our area opened and closed frequently. Our favourite burger place in Seogwipo was incredibly popular, but to our surprise it suddenly closed. The same happened to the very successful pizza restaurant close to the GEC. In this case the owner had trouble finding servers and had to close.

It was a bit of a gamble when we decided to eat out. The hours restaurants held were not regular or predictable. I used my notepad to record what days our favourite places were closed. Sunday, Monday, and Tuesday were common closing days, but a burger place that only sold four types of burgers, French fries, and onion rings closed on Thursday. On the days it was open, this restaurant took two-hour lunch breaks with last orders for dinner taken at six thirty. The burger place was on social media and a popular destination. Korean travelers were often victim of the Thursday closing and long afternoon breaks. This made me feel a lot better as I stood looking at the closed sign.

A popular sushi stop was the American Sushi Roll located on a coastal road. The sushi rolls were consistent and if you were lucky you could see a large pod of dolphins feeding close to the shoreline. A custom in Korean restaurants was to give a complimentary serving of food to valued customers. When we went to the American Sushi Roll with Kate and Kerry the owner gave us a cooked salmon head. When we went as a couple Michael and I received a sample of our favourite sashimi rolls or tempura vegetables.

Jeju Island was known for its black pork from a pig which was smaller than western domestic pig breeds. Its meat had a distinct fattiness that Koreans loved. The owners of the black pork restaurant close to us had connections to the black pork farms on the island. One day we saw piglets in an enclosure as we walked into the restaurant. The piglets were very cute, but regrettably bound for the grill in a year.

Next door to the pork barbecue was a sushi restaurant. An aerated tank by the entrance to the restaurant was full of fish destined for dinner plates. Michael and I called this restaurant "Baby Bunny Sushi." We had assumed that pictures of bunnies on banners were incorporated into the name, but this was not the case. The restaurant's name, "Sushi House", was so obvious other friends used the fact that they used wooden platters to distinguish it from other sushi restaurants in the area.

******

Teaching at BHA

Working at Branksome Hall Asia was restorative for me. An accredited International Baccalaureate (IB) school from kindergarten to grade twelve, I felt the change in educational philosophy from teacher-centred to student-centred learning immediately. The collaborative nature of the teachers and the focus on what was best for the student felt like an old friend returning. The learning environment was a symbiotic mentorship, a collaborative discussion between teacher and student. In staff meetings, my lived experiences and educational background were valued.

Branksome Hall Asia was technologically advanced and all students and staff received an Apple laptop from the school to be returned on departure. Google and other educational platforms were used to enhance teaching and learning in the classroom. There were four software management systems to learn when I arrived. This number decreased to two after a few years due to complaints by teachers. My department head told me to focus on teaching and I learnt the computer systems as the year progressed. Good advice. Learning to navigate the Apple operating system was challenging in the beginning. My biggest challenge was to master the two-finger swipe and retrieve my working desktop.

The science department had two excellent technicians who set up experiments and cleaned the equipment afterwards. They maintained equipment and replaced chemicals when needed. Procuring science books and equipment was an easy task, but importing electronics from overseas was not. Korean customs stopped all electronics which were usually denied entry. The technicians were irreplaceable for their troubleshooting abilities. They found local sources for electronics so we would not have to negotiate with customs.

Like many international schools, the main chemical storage room had no windows or ventilation to the outside. Volatile organic chemical odors were present though not as strong as the room in the UAE. What was different was that the department head quickly ordered new storage cabinets with filters. The chemicals were reorganized using Phillip Harris and UK health and safety guidelines were initiated. A larger cabinet for the more volatile chemicals was purchased and put into a classroom to be vented outside. Initially the vent went through a window. In the summer, holes were made in the wall and the venting was made permanent. The air quality of the storage room improved immediately and the technicians were very appreciative of the changes to their workspace.

******

Working with like-minded colleagues was fulfilling professionally. I became the head of science in my second year. My colleagues and I made the department a better place for students and teachers. As a result, our science exam outcomes were above the world averages in chemistry, biology, physics, and environmental systems and societies. Amazing achievements considering most students were not native English speakers.

Classroom management was never an issue in Korea. Parents believed that education was important and respected the knowledge of teachers. Incidents of misbehavior could be counted on one hand and most included not handing work in on time. Most years I only raised my "teacher voice" once or twice—a completely different classroom environment compared to the Middle East.

As advisors we needed to encourage students to get enough sleep and to stop breaking into the school to complete work. Within the classroom it was difficult to get students to answer direct questions. If their answers were incorrect, they would lose face with their cohort. To work around this, I asked open-ended questions that had many correct answers. Even so, it took a while to gain their trust.

******

Honesty

There was little theft in Korea and the chance of being a victim of crime was minimal. Surveillance cameras were placed at intersections and along main traffic routes as well as at airports, and bus and train stations. In addition, all apartment complexes had high tech cameras monitoring hallways as well as the license plates of cars entering and leaving the complexes.

An honest and hardworking people, Koreans went out of their way to return lost items. One day I dropped a black winter scarf on the way home and thought that I would never see it again. But, as I walked to school the next day, there it was hanging in a place easily seen by anyone walking by. Someone had found it on the ground and placed it at eye level to make it easier for the owner to find.

Valuable items were commonly left on tables and benches for short periods of time with no fear of them being taken. At school, mobile phones, computers, and wallets were left in plain sight on tables in the cafeteria. The idea that someone might steal their possessions was not part of the students' reality. Their trust in the honesty of others was a problem when the grade nine students traveled to Canada for a three-week exchange. Michael called an emergency meeting when he saw that students were leaving their bags unattended in the hotel foyer. Canadians are generally honest, but there was a section of society that took advantage of unattended valuables. The students had to be made aware of this fact.

Our complete trust in the honesty of Korean society was demonstrated by the fact that we did not blink or have any second thoughts when the Covid-19 testing nurse ran off with our passports, our Alien Registration cards, and Michael's credit card at the Covid-19 testing site. We had no doubt that she would bring them back once the forms had been processed— that is exactly what happened.

******

Retirement- Buying land and building a house

We enjoyed living on Jeju Island and I loved working at Branksome Hall Asia. Michael and I entertained the idea of going to another international posting, but we were not as adventurous as we once were. Living in a big city with poor air quality was not an option and we did not wish to repeat our Bangladesh or UAE experiences. European countries as well as China had employment age limits for expatriates and I was approaching sixty. Two of my friends in their late fifties went to recruitment fairs confident they would be hired because there were a multitude of job vacancies. Neither received job offers and they were forced to retire from international teaching before they were ready. Another factor we had to consider was that our parents were growing older, and spending time with them was becoming more important.

Considering all these factors Michael and I continued working at Branksome Hall Asia until it was financially viable to move back to British Columbia. Our brief return to British Columbia in 2013 had demonstrated that our house in Comox was not big enough for our possessions and it had no workshop space for Michael. With the idea of designing and building a house that would suit us we looked online for small acreages north of Victoria.

******

Buying our five-acre building lot on Salt Spring Island was straight forward as we were in Canada at the time. Selling our condominium apartments to release their equity was not. We were in Korea for that transaction. The transfer of ownership documents required our signatures to be witnessed by a lawyer or notary. Korea did not have notaries and the lawyer we found to witness our signatures required that the documents be translated into Korean even though we were signing Canadian documents.

The school's human resources department found a professional service to translate the documents. When they were ready we drove to Jeju city with a Korean friend to act as an interpreter. I thought it would be a quick appointment. After all, the lawyer only had to witness our signatures and verify our identity, but this was not the case.

The Canadian requirement of authenticating signatures on property transfers was not familiar to the Koreans and our friend had difficulty explaining what we needed. The three legal assistants in the office were busy stamping huge piles of documents with different colored stamps and were not that enthusiastic about helping us. We waited patiently and finally one took our passports and Alien Registration cards as well as various pages of the transaction documents to be photocopied. When they returned, we signed the places that had been marked by our lawyer in Canada.

At this point we discovered that land transfers in Korea required the seller to pay a percentage fee on the value of the transaction and the legal assistants thought that each signature was a transaction. We rectified the misunderstanding. Two hours after we arrived at the office a lawyer came down from his office and stamped and sealed with wax the pages that he signed. Though the cost was more than we expected to pay, the final document was very beautiful and official looking with all the seals and ribbons. I hoped the people who received it in Canada appreciated the uniqueness as much as we did.

******

With the condominium sale completed Michael and I designed the layout of our house using a software program. We melded all the good features of the places we had lived in over the years. High ceilings, large open living spaces, no stairs, and lots of windows. The process of designing and redesigning took us most of the winter. A visit to the land in the summer of 2018 helped us decide where we would place the house.

The foundations were dug in the spring of 2019 and we added our sweat equity to the project during our summer vacation. For four weeks we lived in a large canvas tent on the property. We painted walls, laid wooden floors and filled three dumpsters full of house construction waste. Even with our labour the construction costs were over the original budget. To earn additional funds we signed contracts for the 2020-2021 year at Branksome Hall Asia. Not wishing to leave the house vacant we hired a rental agency to find a tenant and look after any issues that might arise.

We did not return to Canada in the summer of 2020 due to pandemic lockdowns and cancelled flights. As Michael and I walked the country roads of Jeju Island we realized that our desire to travel and see the world had diminished considerably. There were not that many places left for us to visit as we had traveled extensively in the seventeen years we had been overseas. From Moscow we had flown to Italy, Spain, Portugal, France, Germany, Greece, the Netherlands, England, Scotland and Ireland for holidays and many others for sports events. While in Bangladesh we traveled to Bali, Cambodia, Nepal, Bhutan, and India. From Thailand we traveled to New Zealand at Christmas and spent shorter holidays golfing locally. The years we spent in the United Arab Emirates allowed us to return to Europe (Turkey, Italy, France, Czech Republic, and Poland) as well as visiting Oman. And finally, while in Jeju we returned to Thailand, visited Australia twice, flew to Japan as well as visited my parents in New Zealand. When I last counted, Michael and I successfully travelled to over forty-two countries. We had accomplished our goal to see the world and it was time to repatriate and reconnect with our families and friends.

Michael and I officially retired from international teaching and returned to Canada on July 1st, 2021. We moved into our custom-built house on Salt Spring Island and unpacked our possessions. Four cubic meters arrived from Korea and we retrieved the rest from the storage room where it had been since 2014. Our Thai furniture was placed where it was designed to go and Russian paintings filled the walls. Our house was perfect but unforeseen allergies made it necessary to move once again. In 2022 we returned to where we started, the Comox Valley on Vancouver Island.

******

Chapter 7:
Dentists, doctors and online learning 2004-2021

Dentists and teeth cleaning

Michael and I endured some strange and very painful teeth cleaning experiences in the years we lived overseas. In Canada we had our teeth cleaned routinely as a benefit of our extended health benefits. Bi-annual cleanings were recommended by our dentists. We liked getting our teeth cleaned hoping it would prevent cavities and gum disease.

In Moscow we asked our colleagues if they knew of a place that cleaned teeth. Our Russian friends did not know what a teeth cleaning was and could not understand why we wanted to go to the dentist voluntarily. They only went when it was necessary. We eventually found a dentist office that advertised a hygienist and made appointments. We expected Canadian hygienist to know what they were doing as they were licenced, but we discovered that this was not the case in Russia.

The dentist's office was in a newer building downtown and it had the familiar feel of a western dentist's office. The brochure advertised the newest and greatest technology to clean teeth which was the ultrasonic scaling method. When I sat in the familiar dental hygienist chair one hygienist covered me with a large plastic covering while the other set up the equipment. After a few minutes I started to think that the two hygienists did not know what they were doing. Water was sprayed everywhere and it was more painful than I expected. The hygienists were having serious conversations and looking worriedly at my top front teeth.

One of the hygienists ran off to get some material that they put on my gum line. The periodontal dressing was necessary as the hygienist had removed gum tissue by leaving the ultrasonic water picks on the area for too long. I was instructed to wear the dressing on my gums for two days. No long-term damage resulted, but when I told my Canadian hygienist she was appalled. She could not understand why untrained people would be allowed to operate the machine.

We made annual teeth cleaning appointments for when we returned to Canada in the summer. At these appointments it was common for the hygienist to recommend more frequent cleanings. I had to educate them about the reality of living outside of Canada. Trained hygienists and a culture that supported them did not exist in many countries.

We did not hear of any reputable dentists or hygienist while in Dhaka and thankfully we did not need one during those years. Thailand was known as a place to get cheap tooth implants, but there were no dental hygienists in Chiangmai. Our friends recommended a dentist that scaled teeth. Unfortunately, her technique was so rough that my jaw was sore for days afterwards—an experience I did not want repeated, so we were back to annual cleanings.

The medical services in Ras Al Khaimah were like those in Bangladesh. Luckily we did not need a doctor, but I broke a molar while eating walnuts and a local friend recommended their dentist. Michael and I located the building downtown, but had difficulty finding the entrance to the dentist office. All the signs to the various businesses were in Arabic. Luckily, we saw a picture in the foyer which had the universal dentist tooth logo and floor number beside it.

Walking into the dentist's office was like stepping back in time. The small waiting room was filled with people, but I was taken to see the dentist immediately. I assumed this was because I was either white, wealthy, or deemed to be an emergency. The large dentist's room was lined with tables cluttered with files and equipment. The chair in the center was at least thirty years old with a spitting sink on the side.

The dentist spoke fluent English and had trained in the United Kingdom, so my anxiety decreased substantially. He told me that my back molar was broken, but he could fix it without a root canal or crown. I prepared myself for the freezing needle, but to my amazement he started grinding the edges to prepare the tooth for the filling immediately. The procedure did not hurt, which made me wonder how often I had been given freezing for no reason. When the filling fell out a year later the dentist replaced it with a different amalgam for free.

When the Covid-19 pandemic of 2020 started we could not return to Canada in the summer. Fortunately, a new dentist office had opened in the GEC about five minutes from the school. A few of our friends had gone for dental work and told us that there were hygienists there as well. We went in person to book appointments. We found a modern facility where the receptionist spoke English.

It had been fifteen years since my Moscow experience and I trusted that the Korean dental system had a more rigorous training and licensing procedure. My hygienist used the newest ultrasonic machine. Other than the towel across my face and not understanding the Korean instructions for what to do with the suction tube the cleaning was successful with no need for dressings or painkillers.

The social bantering that was common in our Canadian cleanings did not occur. The language barrier hindered one-way gossip about general life on the island. The cost of the cleaning in Korea was inexpensive compared to the cost in Canada. Finally, in our last year of international teaching we were able to get our teeth cleaned every six months.

******

Doctors and Hospitalizations

Michael and I were healthy with no underlying medical issues when we started our overseas teaching careers. Not knowing what medical services were going to be available we prepared a first aid kit. The medications included a supply of antibiotics to treat obvious infections. The antibiotics we used for sinus and tonsil infections were easily replaced in Bangladesh, Thailand, and the UAE, as these countries sold antibiotics over the counter.

A small centrally located European Medical Center was used by most of our friends in Moscow. It was set up for expatriates and the doctors spoke English. Only American citizens had access to the Embassy run American Medical Clinic. Michael and I visited a friend admitted to this clinic for abdominal pain.

Had our friend had been critically ill; she would have been medevacked to Europe.

******

There were four types of dengue fever and Michael got his first one while on holiday in Egypt. He was bitten by mosquitoes carrying the virus while we waited in the lobby of a posh hotel in Aswan. After returning to Moscow Michael developed an incredibly high fever and excruciating muscular pain all over his body. After four days of high fevers and muscle pain Michael got better. We did not realize it was dengue until we were describing the symptoms to my father. He had seen the disease in Uganda when my family had lived there in the mid-1960s. Dengue was called "breakbone fever" in Africa as the pain was like having your muscles and joints pulled apart.

In Bangladesh mosquitoes carried dengue or malaria depending on where you lived. Dhaka had dengue mosquitoes and we slept under a mosquito net and had screens on our windows to avoid being bitten. Mosquito spray was a deterrent, but not always effective in preventing bites. Michael and I were frequently bitten at the Australian club. Their restaurant bar was outside and Michael was certain that he got his second case of dengue fever from a mosquito bite received at this establishment.

The Dhaka symptoms were different from the Egyptian dengue. Michael had flu-like symptoms and was very tired. He thought it was only a bad cold and continued to work. On the third day of the illness the principal saw how weak he was and sent him to the hospital emergency. His blood test results confirmed he had hemorrhagic dengue, a life-threatening version of the virus. When I visited that afternoon, he had the trademark petechial rash on his hands and arms and his white cells, hemoglobin, and platelets were all critically low.

The only treatment plan for dengue was bedrest and intravenous fluids. His doctor refused to order Tylenol for his headache; they did not want to damage his liver. Michael stayed in the hospital for four days to monitor the levels of red and white blood cells. As his results improved slowly, neither platelets nor a blood transfusion were required. He was discharged, but daily blood tests were required for a week after discharge to make sure all was in order.

******

In November of 2018, Michael and I flew to Chiangmai for a holiday. Thailand was experiencing a dengue fever outbreak and we were exposed again. The symptoms of Michael's third case of dengue fever appeared within two weeks of our return to Jeju Island. The muscle pain and fever were like those he had with his Egyptian dengue and we treated it as such. Michael was not sick enough to be hospitalized, but he felt horrible and traveling to Canada for the winter break was not pleasant. On the Jeju Seoul leg the attendant was quite concerned with Michael's color and asked if we needed a doctor.

On our return to Korea Michael was not coughing, but had back pain which we attributed to lifting our suitcases. The pain was not behaving like a muscle pull—painkillers did not work and it got worse when he breathed deeply. We decided to go to the emergency in Jeju where a doctor examined Michael, ordered an IV, ECG, blood work, and sent him for a chest x-ray and CAT scan. He was given IV morphine for the pain to improve his breathing. Diagnosed with bacterial pneumonia and a pleural effusion, Michael was admitted to a six-bed surgical ward within a few hours of our arrival.

Michael spent ten days in the Korean hospital receiving intravenous antibiotics and painkillers. When Michael was admitted on Saturday night there was only one other patient in the room. Michael learned the word for pain, but otherwise used miming and the translation app on his phone to ask for things and understand what the doctor was saying.

By Monday the other beds were occupied and the room was full of relatives. Relatives were needed by patients as there were no paid nursing assistants in the Korean system. Whoever was available provided basic care to their relatives in the hospital. They put down sleeping mats on the floor to provide twenty-four-hour care. As I was not there to help him Michael's roommates' relatives returned his food trays and brought him glasses of water the first day.

Michael's condition improved quickly, and he was able to look after himself by the second day. To get new pajamas and bedding he had to walk to the nursing station and ask for them. Once his sheets were changed, he deposited the dirty laundry down the laundry chute in the supply room. He also returned his food trays to the collection racks.

The six-bed ward was noisy and not very relaxing due to the interactions between the relatives, patients and nurses. We asked for a private room so Michael could prep his classes for the cover teacher and watch English movies.

******

I had my own experiences with the Korean medical system. I used the drop-in doctor's office in the GEC to get antibiotics for sinus infections and other issues that required prescription drugs. The doctor used modern scoping equipment to look up my nose and ordered tests and medications after consulting his computer.

In 2020 I woke up with pain in my right shoulder. I initially blamed the screen golf we had played the day before. As the day progressed the pain shifted to my right upper abdomen and became unbearable. Thinking that it could be pneumonia or something worse we drove to the hospital in Jeju. After a chest x-ray, CAT scan and blood tests, my results indicated a massive infection and the likely culprit was my gallbladder.

I was admitted to a five-bed medical ward with intravenous painkillers and started on antibiotics. As I was able to look after myself physically, Michael drove home. My roommates' relatives were happy to help me find things and we communicated using mime and a translate app. The nurses were not fluent in English though there was one day-shift nurse who spoke it well enough to explain things. The doctor drew pictures and I depended on my own nursing knowledge to understand what was going on with my diagnosis and treatment. I was not allowed to eat anything and an intravenous bag of white liquid replaced the nutrients I would normally have eaten.

My symptoms improved quickly and I was given a bowl of broth on the third evening. The next day I was given a breakfast of pork stir fry, a lunch of chicken stir fry, and dinner of a bony fish. Each of these meals was accompanied by kimchi choices and a large bowl of rice. When a bony fish appeared for breakfast the next day, I understood Michael's need for bakery goods and pizza during his ten-day hospital stay. I was discharged on the morning of the fifth day and I had no complaints about the quality of my care.

******

The schools we worked at provided private medical insurance and some policies were better than others. Negotiating the paperwork required by private health insurance packages was challenging. I had no previous experience with paying for a doctor's visit or treatment and claiming the fee back from insurance companies. The Canadian healthcare system was universal, accessible, and supported by taxes. Doctors billed the provincial governments directly for the service they provided and every resident of Canada had access to the services. The only time money exchanged hands was for non-essential cosmetic surgery or other treatments not covered by the medical system. Canadians were proud of the medical system and the cost of a procedure was never a factor in deciding what needed to be done or if it would be done.

With private health coverage we paid the clinic or hospital bill at the time of treatment and then claimed for a reimbursement. Even when covered by a policy reimbursement was only 90% of the original cost. Michael's hospital stay in Dhaka cost us $500.00 USD a day. The total fee for all care and procedures needed to be paid on discharge. Ninety percent of the total was reimbursed by the medical insurance policy, but the money arrived a few months after his discharge. To avoid this financial hit in Korea, we chose to go to the hospital in Jeju that directly billed the medical insurance company the ninety percent. We paid the remaining ten percent when discharged.

What surprised me the most about the private-for-profit medical insurance system was that medications were prescribed that were not necessary. Michael, who was not taking any medications, was discharged with prescriptions to reduce anxiety and prevent stomach ulcers. When a friend slipped on the stairs and bumped his head, he had a full workup including a CAT scan. The doctor found nothing to be concerned about, but still prescribed new medications that interacted with some of the pills he was on for blood sugar control. When he consulted his personal doctor in Australia, they told him not to take any of the new ones.

******

Transition to online learning

The relationship between Chechnya, a republic within the Russian Federation, and the government in Moscow was politically volatile. When we started teaching in Moscow the 2002 Chechen theatre hostage situation was fresh in everyone's minds and security at metro stations was high. If the police suspected a person was from that area, they were asked to produce their passports and the papers required to travel within Russia.

The Beslan hostage situation initiated by Chechen terrorists occurred the year we arrived and ended with the massacre of 333 adults and children in the school. Even though Beslan was thousands of kilometers away Moscow's anti-terrorism measures increased substantially. The governing body of the Anglo-American school voted to improve security at the school as well.

Over the summer holidays a delta barrier was built into the road leading up to the main entrance. The purpose was to block any hostile vehicles driving towards the school. Teachers received ID cards and were required to sign in and out electronically. Visitors were asked to report to the main administration desk to sign in. The appropriate administrator would then escort them around the school as needed. Unusual at the time, these security practices are found in most international schools today.

The school's budget included a defence fund to evacuate teachers and continue to pay salaries if terrorist activities forced the closure of the building. The board expected teachers to continue teaching classes online. Our instructions were to prepare for a lockdown that could last for weeks or months. These were the early days of using technology in the classroom. Only a few international schools had true one-to-one laptop programs used for direct instruction.

The Anglo-American School had internal software systems for attendance, curriculum, and grading, but there was no online course management system. The only platform for classroom lessons was the email system and parents had accounts provided by the school. In those days most students did not have personal computers, tablets, or smart phones. Search engines were in their infancy. I compared the internet to a library with all the books on the floor—it was difficult finding things quickly. Teaching online would have been a challenge; luckily it did not need to be tested while we were in Moscow.

******

The technology to teach online existed at universities to serve students who could not be on campus. I completed my post-diploma nursing degree in Victoria while continuing to work in Comox. We recognized the potential of these online teaching tools at the middle and high school levels. Michael and I completed Masters of Online Teaching Certificates through the University of Illinois during our third and fourth years at Moscow. The courses in this program taught us how to set up hybrid online classrooms where materials and tasks were put online, but face to face instruction occurred in the classroom.

Hybrid classes required that students have equal access to computers at home. The Anglo-American School of Moscow was reluctant to invest in a one-to-one laptop program to ensure this access. The decision limited the application of online learning activities for years in Moscow. Regardless, I managed to create limited online classrooms for my grade six and eight classes. We used the library computers to research and create power point presentations. The finished projects were stored online and accessible through my classroom computer.

Branksome Hall Asia embraced the use of technology within the classroom. The students at Branksome Hall Asia had multiple devices such as computers, tablets, and smartphones to access the internet. Students received instructions face-to-face, and assignments and teaching documents were put into online learning platforms such as google classroom. In many cases the assignments were completed online so students could not "lose" them.

Due to the hybrid structure of my science and biology classrooms the switch to complete online teaching during the Covid-19 pandemic was seamless. Face-to-face classes shifted quickly into online Google-meet classes. Students completed their assignments at home and posted them online. The move to complete online learning in 2020 was necessitated by a global pandemic rather than a war or terrorist attack which I had originally been preparing for in 2004.

******

Final words

As an overview of our seventeen years overseas I have the following to say about the schools I worked at. The Anglo-American school of Moscow had a very good salary and benefit package. The educational philosophy of the people we worked with complemented ours. The students were from all over the world and this created a multicultural and dynamic environment with the common language being English.

When in Moscow I became head of middle school science. I promoted inquiry-based learning lessons in the grade six to eight curriculum. The middle school results on a USA science based standardized test improved over the next four years. Michael and I enjoyed the culture and history of Moscow. This kept us there for a fifth year even though the leadership of the school had pigeon-holed us. We left with over a hundred pictures and multiple pieces of folk art such as carved and painted boxes.

Bangladesh offered us the career choices we wanted and a decent pay package. The school culture was supportive and the International Baccalaureate Program matched our philosophy of teaching and learning. It was a smaller school than Moscow and not as well resourced. We disagreed with the new principal's ideas frequently as they were UK centric, but the opportunity to work with expert teachers was fulfilling. Most of the students were Bangladeshi and my techniques for teaching students who were learning English improved. The international school mantra was that we were all English teachers independent of what subject we taught.

When living in Bangladesh I witnessed extreme poverty and government corruption, which resulted in a lack of universal energy supplies and clean water, as well as generalized lawlessness. I will never forget the horror of being the victim of a premeditated armed assault. Souvenirs of our two years in Bangladesh included hand printed material, brass fish, curtains, and tablecloths.

Michael and I accepted the job in Thailand rather than return to Canada. The American Pacific International School's salary package was modest, but the location was beautiful. The owners' actions and inability to acknowledge the value of qualified teachers did not support educational outcomes and job satisfaction. On the positive side the students were a pleasure to teach. The Thai culture supported teachers with celebrations like Wai Kru day at the beginning of the year that focused on the significance of the relationship between student and teachers.

Michael and I enjoyed working in Chiangmai. Living on campus away from the city was a welcome change from the overcrowded noisy and polluted streets of Dhaka. What we gained from living in Thailand were memories of time spent with colleagues and visiting friends and family. We purchased teak furniture, ceramics and wood carvings which filled our Canadian home.

The pay and benefit package at Ras Al Khaimah Academy enticed us to accept the positions rather than remain in Canada. Any income was better than no income and moving to the United Arab Emirates gave Michael an administrative role which he enjoyed. Living in the desert was sandy and hot and there was not much to do socially other than play golf. The school's ethos did not match my fundamental values of autonomy and fairness and I left to find a better workplace.

Branksome Hall Asia in South Korea had an excellent pay package and their International Baccalaureate curriculum was well developed and rigorous. Students and parents were committed and focused on achieving top grades and their desire to be successful academically kept us busy. Teaching in Korea gave me the greatest professional satisfaction. As head of the science department, I worked with my colleagues to create lessons that promoted student motivated learning. The success of our graduating higher-level biology and environmental systems students gave me great satisfaction. In 2021 Branksome Hall Asia ranked in the top 1% of approximately four thousand IBDP schools in the world.

The collaborative nature of a well-run IB school supported individual differences and allowed teachers to complete projects that would have been impossible anywhere else. I created gardens and purchased hydroponic equipment to promote the use of plants in lessons and investigations. My colleagues were innovative, creative, and motivated to design the best learning experiences for students. They became our family and Jeju Island surrounded us with natural beauty.

******

My experiences overseas taught me to react to events and behaviours with an open mind. Whatever came, we ate it. Our host countries usually had completely different ways of looking at things based on their cultural and political history. I concluded that the dichotomies found in Russia and the extreme poverty of Bangladesh could never be remediated by western cultures and it was not our place to do so.

The expat teaching community, though small, was well connected, and Michael and I formed lifelong friendships with many of our teaching colleagues. Email and social media allow us to maintain contact with these friends who are spread around the globe. Our experiences of living and working in various countries remain a shared discourse. My story has detailed day to day events and though a few were extremely difficult emotionally, the good always outweighed the bad. Teaching in the "expat bubble" was definitely never boring.

Acknowledgements

I would like to thank my international teaching friends who participated in my adventures and made them so memorable. A special mention goes to Toni and Kim who inspired me to start writing my stories rather than just tell them over coffee. I must acknowledge Keith for reading my early versions and supporting my desire to publish.

I am indebted to both my parents who instilled the love of travel and adventure into me starting at an early age. My mother died before this book was published, but she read and gave valued feedback on early versions. My father's memoir, *Improbable Journeys,* inspired me to write my own. His persistence in my completing the project was appreciated.

A much appreciated thank-you goes to Ron and Pat Smith for their editing expertise. They helped create a manuscript that held promise. Not to be forgotten, Scott and the team at Friesen Press who made my desire to be published a reality.

Thank you to my supportive siblings, Helen and Patrick as well as my daughter Elizabeth. Finally, I thank my husband Michael, for being so tolerant while I focused on writing and publishing this book and not blinking when the bills for editing and publishing arrived.

Printed in Canada